DISCARDED
—by—
Memphis Public Library

THE PROPER CARE OF AMPHIBIANS
TW-116

Overleaf: *Dendrobates histrionicus.* Photo by K. Lucas, Steinhart Aquarium.

Opposite: *Hyla andersonii.* Photo by R. T. Zappalorti.

The Proper Care of
AMPHIBIANS

John Coborn

© Copyright 1992 by T.F.H. Publications, Inc.

Distributed in the UNITED STATES to the Pet Trade by T.F.H.
Publications, Inc., One T.F.H. Plaza, Neptune City, NJ 07753;
distributed in the UNITED STATES to the Bookstore and Library
Trade by National Book Network, Inc. 4720 Boston Way, Lanham
MD 20706; in CANADA to the Pet Trade by H & L Pet Supplies Inc.,
27 Kingston Crescent, Kitchener, Ontario N2B 2T6; Rolf C. Hagen
Ltd., 3225 Sartelon Street, Montreal 382 Quebec; in CANADA to the
Book Trade by Macmillan of Canada (A Division of Canada Publish-
ing Corporation), 164 Commander Boulevard, Agincourt, Ontario
M1S 3C7; in ENGLAND by T.F.H. Publications, PO Box 15,
Waterlooville PO7 6BQ; in AUSTRALIA AND THE SOUTH PA-
CIFIC by T.F.H. (Australia), Pty. Ltd., Box 149, Brookvale 2100
N.S.W., Australia; in NEW ZEALAND by Ross Haines & Son, Ltd.,
82 D Elizabeth Knox Place, Panmure, Auckland, New Zealand; in
the PHILIPPINES by Bio-Research, 5 Lippay Street, San Lorenzo
Village, Makati, Rizal; in SOUTH AFRICA by Multipet Pty. Ltd., P.O.
Box 35347, Northway, 4065, South Africa. Published by T.F.H.
Publications, Inc. Manufactured in the United States of America by
T.F.H. Publications, Inc.

CONTENTS

Many amphibians, like this southern toad, *Bufo terrestris*, are both attractive and easily maintained in captivity. Photo by R. T. Zappalorti.

Introduction

Amphibian is the familiar collective name given to a member of the class Amphibia, which includes the salamanders and newts, the frogs and toads, and the lesser known limbless caecilians. Amphibians are a relatively small group of vertebrates (with just over 4,000 described species) that are often included together with the reptiles in the study of herpetology. Herpetology (derived from the Greek "herpeton," a creeping thing), is a branch of zoology that deals with the evolution, classification, biology, and distribution of two vertebrate classes, the Amphibia and the Reptilia.

The relatively few people who are fond of crocodiles, snakes, and lizards usually also show a predilection for frogs, toads, and newts, an attitude that the majority of other people find hard to understand. Even Linnaeus, the father of modern zoological classification, indicated a personal loathing for some of the creatures he was classifying, including amphibians. In his *Systema Naturae* he said: "most amphibia are abhorrent because of their cold body, pale color, cartilaginous skeleton, filthy skin, fierce aspect, calculating eye, offensive smell, harsh voice, squalid habitation, and terrible venom; and so their Creator has not exerted his powers to make many of them." A hundred and fifty years later, the herpetologist Hans Gadow wrote in the preface to his *Amphibia and Reptiles* (1901): "One reason for the fact that this branch of Natural History (herpetology), is not very popular, is a prejudice against creatures which are clammy and cold to the touch, and some of them may be poisonous. People who delight in keeping Newts or Frogs, Tortoises or Snakes, are, as a rule, considered eccentric. But in reality these cold-blooded creatures are of fascinating interest provided they are studied properly."

In more recent times herpetologists, both professional and amateur, are found in relatively greater numbers and are on the increase. Improvement in communications through the media has undoubtedly played a major part in this phenomenon. Today, amateur herpetologists are more readily accepted and are considered to be almost as "normal" as sky-divers, shark-catchers, or golf fanatics.

There are a great many herpetologists whose special love is the amphibians, and there are those who delight in keeping them. An expanding interest in wildlife, probably impassioned by the excellent, ever-improving nature films to be seen on TV, has led to an increasing awareness of the need to conserve all species and not just the "cuddly" ones. It is accurate though perhaps ironic to say that some species of amphibians may only be saved from extinction by breeding them in a controlled or captive environment.

Considerable improvements in our knowledge of the captive husbandry and breeding of the amphibians have occurred in the last two or three decades. Although some species have always been reasonably easy to keep alive, successful breeding was a different matter. Other species have formerly been classed as "difficult" or "impossible" to keep. It was the general realization that most amphibians are relatively "non-adaptive" to environmental changes that has vastly improved our chances of not only keeping them alive and healthy but also propagating them. When an amphibian is removed from the wild it must be kept in an environment very similar to that from which it originated, and this must include the appropriate seasonal climatic changes. It is therefore very important to have a detailed knowledge of the natural habitat of a species, and the means to reproduce it, before any attempt is made to keep it in the terrarium.

The keeping of amphibians, many of which can be described as living jewels, in the home terrarium is a fascinating hobby and has its

Even salamanders, like this northern dusky salamander, _Desmognathus fuscus fuscus_, can be rewarding pets if given the proper care and attention. Photo by R. T. Zappalorti.

advantages in relation to some of the more conventional mammal or bird pets. Relatively little space is required for a terrarium that can be esthetically pleasing, attractive, and an instant point of conversation whenever visitors arrive. Terraria can be set up complete with plants and animals, thus bringing a little nature into the lives of even those living in city high-rise apartments. Given a few simple requirements, amphibians are clean, odor-free, reasonably quiet, and

Leopard frogs make excellent pets and are readily available in most pet stores. Photo by R. T. Zappalorti.

non-demanding. Once the basics have been set up, maintenance and cleaning chores are minimal and you have every opportunity to do your own research.

This book is designed primarily for the prospective home terrarium keeper, but I have included material that will be of interest to all people concerned with amphibians both in the wild and in captivity. The early chapters deal with general information and care, while the later chapters briefly describe a selection of species. The species sections are not intended to be a taxonomic reference or even a field guide to help enable the reader to identify species—that is outside the scope of this book. Information on positive identification should be gleaned from original descriptions or from a good field guide. The present text is intended purely to demonstrate the infinite variety of shape, pattern, color, habits, etc., which occurs in the amphibian world and to present some guidelines on the care of some individuals or groups of species. In particular, the whole text has been designed to promote or enhance the enthusiasm of the reader for this fascinating subject. I have endeavored to include all information that will enable the beginner to learn about amphibians, to set up his terrarium, obtain his animals, keep them successfully, and, hopefully, to breed them.

Some of the most popular and easy-to-keep frogs are treefrogs, like this *Leptopelis natalensis*. Photo by K. H. Switak.

Understanding Amphibians

MYTHS, LEGENDS, AND ATTITUDES

Frogs, toads, and salamanders were creeping upon the earth's surface for millions of years before the human race evolved. Indeed, when the ancestors of man appeared some 2.5 million years ago, amphibians had already reached a stage of evolution similar to that found in the contemporary species.

Early man had little knowledge of science; his prime purposes in life were to survive and to reproduce. His fellow animals were probably regarded only as items of food or dangerous adversaries. The fact that many amphibians are poisonous or bitter to the taste probably has a bearing on the many attitudes, myths, and legends pertaining to them. Although our knowledge of the natural sciences has increased many thousand-fold in recent years, these attitudes still persist in many sections of the community, even in parts of the so-called "civilized" nations. In fact, the sections of the community that considered themselves to be more "civilized and intelligent" have come up with the most colorful stories.

In the Bible we can encounter references to frogs in one of the plagues of Egypt and to frogs and toads being vomited up by the apocalyptic dragon (possibly based on the fact that snakes and lizards will sometimes regurgitate a meal, for one reason or another).

William Shakespeare (1546-1616), the great English dramatist and poet, was one of the first to bring an amphibian into popular literature when he wrote the lines (*As You Like It*, Act II, Scene I): "Sweet are the uses of adversary Which, like the toad, ugly and venomous, Wears yet a precious jewel in its head."

Toads have been widely misunderstood throughout the years. Many unsubstantiated rumors, such as the classic about how they cause warts on the human skin, have been immensely blown out of proportion. Photo of *Bufo bufo* by L. Wischnath.

Early Europeans really did believe that the toad possessed a precious jewel inside its head (this myth probably arose from the fact that the toad has a glittering, golden iris). Unfortunately, the jewel could only be obtained by removing it from a live toad; thus the jewel never actually came into anyone's possession as the toad invariably died before it could be extracted!

Even some of our pioneer taxonomists and herpetologists seem to have had but a poor regard for the creatures they were describing. Bernard Lacepede (1756-1825), a pioneer French zoologist, in his *Histoire de Quadrupedes Ovipares et des Serpents* (1789), made the following observations about toads:

"Public opinion has long stigmatized this disgusting beast, whose proximity revolts us...everything about it, its very name is vile....It is surely the fortuitous product of dust and moisture....It seems corrupt in all its parts....It might be molded from a coarse and clammy clay....Its huge belly is always distended....The angry glitter in its eyes is revolting....It has legs, but they do not raise its carcass above the mire; it has eyes but they do not welcome light, its bane. Decaying or poisonous plants are its food, its habitation is filthy, its habits disgusting, its body deformed, its color dingy, its breath foul; it opens its hideous jaws when it is attacked. It has the obstinacy of the stupid. It would seem that Nature has only created the toad to emphasize the beauty and nobility of her other creatures."

Lacepede goes on to make the suggestion that all toads should be exterminated: " Why should this creature which pollutes earth and water, even human beings who look upon it, be allowed to live?"

Another French zoologist, Georges Cuvier (1762-1832), in his *Regne Animal* (1829) declared the toad to be "hideous and revolting," while the earlier Swiss naturalist Conrad Gesner (1516-1565) in his *Historia Animalium* (1559-1586) suggested that "its glance is enough to make a man turn pale and ill."

Along with the toad, the salamanders were endowed

The word "salamander" is Greek for "fire animal" and is probably born from certain myths about the salamander's "incendiary capabilities," all of which are totally untrue. Photo by M. Gilroy.

with some truly amazing attributes. Most of these early myths pertained to the European spotted or "fire" salamander. The word salamander itself is derived from a Greek word meaning "fire animal," and most myths are related to its incendiary talents. Not only is it "born of the fire," it is impervious to fire, it requires it for nourishment, and can even extinguish it if necessary! The salamander's fire connection probably is based on a certain amount of fact. Being a somewhat reclusive creature that spends its days holed up in rotting logs, it would have frequently been inadvertently transported along with the fuel for early fireplaces. As the heat of the fire reached the center of the log, a trapped salamander would, not unreasonably, have made an attempt to escape, giving the impression that it was born of the fire. If the fire was not a successful one, this of course could be blamed on the salamander's extinguitory talents.

Although modern zoologists show a more benign attitude toward the creatures they study, a mixed regard for the lowly animals is still apparent in the average person. Apart from those sensible and forward-thinking people who have an interest in frogs and toads, salamanders and newts, the majority either dismiss them as being of no importance whatsoever or show a definite loathing toward them. The "facts" that they are cold and slimy, live in swamps, and are undoubtedly poisonous lead the major part of the human race to have a very low opinion of them. The relatively small (but growing) number of people who keep and study the lowly creatures are still regarded with a certain amount of suspicion by their contemporaries but perhaps not quite as much as a few decades ago.

Through the efforts of advanced public education, many poor attitudes toward certain amphibians are finally starting to be reversed. The photo shown is of *Scaphiopus hammondi* by J. K. Langhammer.

CONSERVATION

Of all classes of vertebrate animals, the amphibians seem to have suffered the most in recent decades. Many older people can relate to this, especially those who as children collected frog eggs, have decreased in numbers by from 50% to 100%. In other words, certain species in Europe, North America, and other industrialized areas have become extinct in particular areas or, at best, have become exceedingly rare.

If habitat destruction continues at its present rate, even abundant species like this northern leopard frog, *Rana pipiens,* may have trouble surviving. Photo by A. Norman.

tadpoles, or adult frogs and newts. Forty years ago the numbers of frogs and toads to be found seemed to have been infinite, but today most of these have disappeared. Populations of amphibians

What has contributed to this decline? There are a number of factors that can be considered.

Habitat Destruction

During the fifties through to the seventies reclamation of

Small amphibians like these ensatinas, *Ensatina eschscholtzii,* are quite delicate and do not take to man's destructive tendencies very well. Photo by K.Lucas, Steinhart Aquarium.

wetlands became something of a fashion. Reclaimed land could be used for forestry, agriculture, residential housing, or industry. There was no thought for the amphibians or other creatures that depend on wetlands to be able to survive. Fortunately the last two decades have seen widespread recognition that wetlands are ecologically important; however, in some areas it is already too late. Destruction of forests, heathlands, and other habitats for similar reasons to those above have contributed to the decline of many species. What is required is a general international strategy to control the environment and to maintain its ecology intact by balanced use of the land.

Pollution

Chemical effluents released from factories or as by-products of mining, etc., have had a dramatic destructive effect on aquatic life at various times and locations. The

Tiger salamanders, *Ambystoma tigrinum*, make hardy captives, but are not often seen for sale. Photo by R. T. Zappalorti.

problem has been more or less alleviated in many countries that have brought in strict legislation on the disposal of industrial effluents. However, this kind of pollution must still be regarded as a serious threat to amphibian populations in many parts of the world. Acid rain caused by the drift of industrial smoke containing sulfurous gases is another factor contributing to the demise of amphibian populations. An even more serious threat probably is the use of biocides and inorganic fertilizers in agriculture. Biocides include herbicides (weed killers) and insecticides, which are in some cases so potent as to kill amphibians directly. They are also killed indirectly by the destruction of prey insects and by the destruction of vegetative cover. Biocides and fertilizers can destroy aquatic life by dramatically altering the pH of the water. Many amphibians, particularly the larvae, are unable to tolerate relatively high alkalinity or acidity. Again, progressive societies have tried to address the problem by developing safer chemicals.

Collecting and Trade

The collecting and sale of amphibians for private collections, for research purposes, and for food has, in the past, been a major factor contributing to the demise of wild populations. An anonymous article entitled "The exploitation of reptiles and fish for trade purposes," published in a British scientific journal in 1928, shows that concern was already being expressed at that time. Among other animals, the article reports "tens of thousands of green tree frogs, *Hyla arborea* (one single consignment amounted to 10,000 specimens), hundreds of cave salamanders, *Hydromantes genei* and spectacled salamanders, *Salamandrina terdigitata* were imported into England." More recently it was estimated that between 1968 and 1970 some 96,190 specimens of salamanders and newts, and a massive 47,050,500 frogs and toads were collected in Italy for commercial, scientific, and culinary purposes! These are mere examples of the potential destructive power of over-collection. Fortunately, legislation in most countries has now regulated the trade of many species thought to be endangered.

Introduced Species

Introduction of non-native animal species to new areas can have a negative effect on the native wildlife, including amphibians. Thus fish introduced for economic purposes will soon destroy an amphibian breeding habitat. Even domestic cats and other predatory animals will take their toll. The mongoose, introduced to some areas to control snakes, is also a major predator of amphibians. In Italy, introduced pheasants have contributed to the demise of several frog species by eating tadpoles and froglets. Even non-native amphibians themselves can be a threat to native species. In Switzerland, introduced marsh frogs, *Rana ridibunda*, have displaced populations of native green frogs (*R. esculenta* and *R. lessonae*). Bullfrogs, *R. catesbeiana*, from Louisiana were introduced into northern Italy between 1932 and 1937. They have now become well established and have displaced several native species in some areas. Another example is the introduction of the marine toad, *Bufo marinus* to Queensland, Australia (where it is known as the "cane toad"), also in the 1930's, ostensibly to control pests of the sugar cane. The toads found the conditions so much to their liking that they have been on the increase ever since and are destroying many of the smaller native animals both by directly devouring them and by displacing populations. Ironically, they have never been of much use in the job for which they were introduced.

EVOLUTION OF THE AMPHIBIA

In order to better understand the status of modern amphibians in zoological classification, it is necessary to have a basic knowledge of their evolution in relation to the other classes of vertebrates (animals possessing a backbone). All of the land-dwelling vertebrates (the reptiles, the birds, and the mammals) owe thanks to our common vertebrate ancestors, the amphibians, for making that gigantic step millions of years ago that led to a life on land. The amphibians arose from certain groups of fishes that had hitherto been the ruling vertebrates. Other than plants, the only living things that had adapted to a life on land previous to amphibians were certain groups of invertebrates. Today's amphibians are the living representatives of the first group of vertebrates to colonize the land. Our present knowledge of evolution is derived from a mixture of theory and fact brought about by the study and comparison of fossil and living forms.

From Water to Land

The transition of vertebrates to life on land from life in the

Most frogs and toads are readily recognized by their greatly developed hind legs, which are modified for jumping. Photo of *Rana ridibunda* by G. Dibley.

water initially required two major adaptations: the ability to breathe atmospheric air and a means of locomotion over the uneven land surface where friction is relatively high. Some of the primitive fishes were already preadapted for breathing atmospheric air as they had previously evolved lungs. It is assumed that, like their modern counterparts the lungfishes, they would have used their lungs for atmospheric air breathing during times of drought.

Locomotion on land was another problem, however, the typical paired fins of the fishes being unsuitable. In water the body of a fish is relatively weightless, but in the less dense medium of air it is necessary for the body to be carried by much stronger and more robust supports capable of holding the body in counter-reaction to gravitational pull and also enabling the animal to propel itself over the land surface. Thus the primitive paired fins of the fishes eventually became modified into limbs with hands and feet.

The First Amphibians

It was probably toward the end of the Devonian period, about 350 million years ago, that the first crossopterygian fishes came out onto the land. It is most likely that these were freshwater rhizodontoid fishes, of which the genus *Eusthenopteron* is of particular importance. *Eusthenopteron* was an elongate, carnivorous fish that was undoubtedly on the direct line toward the early amphibians. In evolutionary terms, the emergence from the water onto land was one of the boldest steps in the history of life and perhaps can be compared with man's first sallies into space, a venturing into a completely new environment. Once the initial step had been made, however, it was not long before these advanced, air-breathing fishes became transformed into primitive amphibians.

Ichthyostega and other early amphibians, although able to breathe air and having legs, were still very fish-like, and it is unlikely that they spent a great deal of time away from the water. However, they had a distinct advantage over the fishes in that they could cross land in search of a new water supply in times of adversity and could thus increase their chances of survival.

In order to spend greater periods of time out of the water, the lungs that had been inherited from the crossopterygian ancestors had to develop to a greater degree of efficiency, although in the larval stage the ichthyostegids still continued to respire by means of gills as most living amphibians still do today. In

A mud-skipper, *Periophthalmus koelreuteri*. Mud-skippers are amphibious fishes that spend much of their time on land. Photo by H. Stultz.

immersed in the water. It is probable that the early amphibians never ventured very far away from the rivers and lakes to which they returned at frequent intervals to replenish the fluids lost through evaporation. Although having developed means of moving about on land, they did not lose the ability to swim quite well, using the paddle-like tail for propulsion and the (sometimes webbed) feet for stabilization. Most modern amphibians still require a wet or at least damp environment in order to survive, though some of them, as we shall see later, have developed some remarkable means of fluid conservation in drought conditions.

fact, the life history of many amphibians can be considered a speedy re-enactment of the evolutionary emergence from water to land. The amphibian larva is virtually an aquatic, gill-breathing fish that metamorphoses into an air-breathing, terrestrial tetrapod.

A further problem that arose for land-dwellers was the possibility of desiccation or drying up. To the fish, this poses no difficulties as it is continually bathed in the fluid in which it lives, but to land-dwelling creatures it is a major problem. The first land dwellers were faced with the necessity of conserving body fluids while no longer

The Age of Amphibians

During the Carboniferous (USA scientists usually split this period into two, the Mississippian and Pennsylvanian) and Permian periods of geological time,

The Ozark hellbender,
Cryptobranchus alleganiensis
bishopi. **Photo by K. T. Nemuras.**

developed tough skins, often underlain by ossicles or bony plates. Thus the outer covering of the body became increasingly efficient in preventing the evaporation of body fluids and shielding the animal from its environment.

The ichthyostegids, which are recognized as forefathers of the more typical amphibians, developed into a number of lines that not only eventually led to our modern amphibians but also radiated into the ancestral lines of the higher vertebrate classes: the reptiles, the birds, and the mammals. Most of the early amphibians were large salamander-like creatures that inhabited the swamps of the Carboniferous period.

starting about 345 million years ago and extending until about 225 million years ago (thus in total for about 120 million years), the amphibians ruled the land where there was no other group of vertebrates in direct competition with them. Many of the first amphibians retained some fish-type scales for protection, and some of the later amphibians, especially during the Permian period,

THE MODERN AMPHIBIANS

Although a considerable amount of fossil amphibian material has been found, there are still many gaps in the fossil record linking the early amphibians with the modern ones, resulting in a great deal of controversy in the theories put forward by scientists. We have a situation in which the modern Amphibia exhibit the following uniting characteristics:

1) The teeth are pedicellate, in which there is a zone of weakness present between the base and the crown.

2) Simple, cylindrical vertebral centra.

3) The skin typically lacks scales and epidermal glands are present, keeping the surface moist for cutaneous respiration, supplementing or replacing the use of lungs.

4) The skull has large openings in the temporal and orbital regions (but not in the very strangely specialized Apoda).

5) The presence of two bones in the middle ear—stapes and operculum—rather than the single stapes characteristic of other lower tetrapods (but again not in the Apoda).

The oldest known caecilians, salamanders, and frogs are very similar to their living descendants. Despite the common uniting characteristics given above, there is no conclusive evidence in any Carboniferous or

Permian amphibian fossils that would indicate these characteristics to have originated from a single common ancestor. The only documented ancestor of modern amphibian lineage which shows direct evidence of ancestry from late Paleozoic amphibians is the (probable) frog ancestor *Triadobatrachus* from the lower Triassic period (about 225 million years ago) of Madagascar.

This photo shows how the Brazilian caecilian *Chthonerpeton viviparum* takes its prey, in this case, a worm. Photo by J. Visser.

Housing

Early attempts to keep amphibians in captivity were fraught with difficulty and often doomed to failure due to an inadequate knowledge of the biological requirements of the species and to a lack of the technology required to reproduce specific life support systems.

The modern terrarium keeper may be thankful to the generations of pioneering aquarists who, after years of trial and error, can now boast the ability to keep and breed almost any species of freshwater fish. There are many parallels between the keeping of fishes and amphibians, particularly with regard to the water content of the terrarium. Indeed, certain totally aquatic amphibians require an aquarium almost identical to that in which fishes are kept.

The beginner to amphibian keeping must first decide what species he wishes to keep, must study the habits and habitat of that species, and then must plan the type of accommodation required. It is a fatal mistake to obtain specimens first and then to panic because the necessary accommodations have to be prepared in a hurry!

Housing for captive amphibians can be loosely divided into three categories:

1. The aquarium—for those species that are totally aquatic and in which there is no provision for a "land" area.

2. The aquaterrarium—for those species that spend varying amounts of time both on land and in water. Ratios of land to water will vary depending on the habits. Most amphibian species will require this type of housing if breeding is to be successful.

3. The terrarium—for those species that are predominantly terrestrial.

In addition to the above, the keen amphibian keeper will store all manner of glass jars, plastic containers, goldfish

The southern leopard frog, *Rana utricularia*, is not a difficult species to house and thus is highly recommended for the beginner. Photo by R. T. Zappalorti.

The African clawed frog, *Xenopus laevis*, is a totally aquatic pet and does extremely well in captivity. Photo by Dr. H. Grier.

bowls, etc., for use as hospital containers, temporary housing, rearing vessels, live-food containers, and so on.

THE AQUARIUM

In this context, the aquarium is a container of water reproducing a totally aquatic environment, with no exposed areas of land, used for totally aquatic amphibia (for example axolotls or *Xenopus*). An aquarium tank may also be used as a terrarium or an aquaterrarium. There are many types of aquarium available on the market, and if

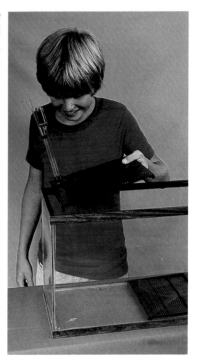

This small boy is showing how to properly place an undergravel filter. Photo by Dr. Herbert R. Axelrod.

you visit your pet shop you may find it difficult to decide what is best for your purposes. Tanks may be made of molded clear plastic or plexiglass. These are usually small (up to a capacity of about 5 gallons or 22.5 liters) and are ideal for rearing larvae or young aquatic amphibians. They are less suited for permanent display tanks as they are usually too small in which to install an attractive aquascape. Regular cleaning will eventually cause the plastic surface to develop an opaque appearance, thus spoiling the view.

Steel-framed aquaria, which were popular with aquarists for many years, are now almost obsolete, though they still have their uses. The disadvantages of such tanks are that the frames will corrode readily unless they are carefully rust-proofed and painted at regular intervals with non-toxic paint, and they

are prone to leaks but can be repaired with silicone sealer. If you have such a tank it is perhaps best to use it as a dry-land terrarium.

The most popular type of aquarium today is without doubt the all-glass tank, which consists of a number of sheets of glass of appropriate sizes cemented together with silicone sealer. Such tanks may be purchased ready-made, and most manufacturers are also willing to make them to specific designs if required.

Substrate Materials and Decoration

Many aquatic amphibians can be kept in almost "clinical" conditions, the animals being simply placed in a tankful of suitable water. Indeed, as long as the tank is kept in a quiet spot and the animals are not subjected to continual disturbance, many species appear to thrive in such circumstances. The species suited to such situations are those most frequently used in laboratory culture for convenience sake as they can be kept with the minimum of hassles.

The display aquarium, however, should be esthetically pleasing. For most small aquatic amphibians, an aquarium can be set up in a similar manner to a fish aquarium (coldwater or tropical, depending on the species), and many tips may be obtained from books about fish-keeping. A natural-looking environment with plants, rocks,

driftwood, etc., will not only be decorative, it will provide the inhabitants with hiding places that will make them secure and more likely to breed.

The best type of substrate for an aquarium is washed river

This photo shows an attractive aquatic substrate/hiding place combination. Photo by R. D. Bartlett.

TROPICAL FISH HOBBYIST
Helping marine, freshwater and herptile hobbyists for 42 years

Temperate Marine Fishes

The Paludarium: A New Challenge

ISSN 0041-3259

Since 1952, *Tropical Fish Hobbyist* has been the source of accurate, up-to-the-minute, and fascinating information on every facet of the aquarium hobby. Join the more than 50,000 devoted readers world-wide who wouldn't miss a single issue.

Subscribe right now so you don't miss a single copy!

Return To:
Tropical Fish Hobbyist, P.O. Box 427, Neptune, NJ 07753-0427
YES! Please enter my subscription to *Tropical Fish Hobbyist*.
Payment for the length I've selected is enclosed. U.S. funds only.

CHECK ONE: ☐ 1 year-$30 ☐ 2 years-$55 ☐ 3 years-$75 ☐ 5 years-$120
12 ISSUES 24 ISSUES 36 ISSUES 60 ISSUES

(Please allow 4-6 weeks for your subscription to start.) *Prices subject to change without notice*

☐ LIFETIME SUBSCRIPTION (max 30 Years) $495
☐ SAMPLE ISSUE $3.50
☐ GIFT SUBSCRIPTION. Please send a card announcing this gift. I would like the card to read: _____
☐ I don't want to subscribe right now, but I'd like to have one of your FREE catalogs listing books about pets. Please send catalog to:

SHIP TO:
Name _____
Street _____ Apt. No. _____
City _____ State _____ Zip _____

U.S. Funds Only. Canada add $11.00 per year; Foreign add $16.00 per year.
Charge my: ☐ VISA ☐ MASTER CHARGE ☐ PAYMENT ENCLOSED

Card Number _____ Expiration Date _____

Cardholder's Name (if different from "Ship to":) _____

Cardholder's Address (if different from "Ship to":) _____

Cardholder's Signature _____

...From T.F.H., the world's largest publisher of bird books, a new bird magazine for birdkeepers all over the world...

CAGED BIRD HOBBYIST
IS FOR EVERYONE
WHO LOVES BIRDS.

CAGED BIRD HOBBYIST
IS PACKED WITH VALUABLE
INFORMATION SHOWING HOW
TO FEED, HOUSE, TRAIN AND CARE
FOR ALL TYPES OF BIRDS.

Subscribe right now so you don't miss a single copy!   SM-316

Return to:
CAGED BIRD HOBBYIST, P.O. Box 427, Neptune, NJ 07753-0427

YES! Please enter my subscription to **CAGED BIRD HOBBYIST**. Payment for the number of issues I've selected is enclosed. *U.S. funds only.

CHECK ONE:	☐ 4 Issues	$9.00
	☐ 12 Issues for the Price of 10	25.00
	☐ 1 Sample Issue	3.00

☐ Gift Subscription. Please send a card announcing this gift.   PRICES SUBJECT TO CHANGE
I would like the card to read _____

_____

☐ I don't want to subscribe right now, but, I'd like to receive one of your FREE catalogs listing books about pets. Please send the catalog to:

SHIP TO:
Name _____ Phone ( )
Street _____
City _____ State _____ Zip _____

U.S. Funds Only. Canada, add $1.00 per issue; Foreign, add $1.50 per issue.

Charge my: ☐ VISA   ☐ MASTER CHARGE   ☐ PAYMENT ENCLOSED

_____
Card Number   Expiration Date

_____
Cardholder's Name (if different from "Ship to:")

_____
Cardholder's Address (if different from "Ship to:")

_____
Please allow 4–6 weeks for your subscription to start.   Cardholder's Signature

sand or gravel, which may be obtained in various grades from your supplier. Although aquarium gravels have usually been cleaned before sale, they may pick up varying amounts of dust and debris depending on the amount of time they have been stored. It is therefore always prudent to rewash the gravel anyway. This is accomplished by putting it in a bucket and swishing a running hose about in it until the

effluent is crystal-clear. To give a more pleasing effect, aquarium gravel is usually sloped from the front of the tank toward the rear. A 5 cm (2 in) depth at the front, rising to about 7.5 cm (3 in) at the rear, is adequate for most smaller tanks.

Rocks and pebbles may be used to vary the aquascape, creating terraces, caves, and valleys. Suitable rocks may be purchased from your pet store; both natural and artificial varieties are often available. Great care should be taken in the selection of artificial rocks (arches, caves, etc.) as, although most of them are perfectly safe to use, there is a danger of upsetting the esthetic appeal of the aquarium by including something that is obviously out of place. The author is definitely against including such artifacts as plastic divers, sunken galleons, and treasure chests! The best kind of rocks to use are those collected from the bed of a clear, running stream. Such rocks will already have been weathered to varying degrees and will look as though they belong in the water. All collected or purchased rocks should be soaked in water containing a small amount of bleach for 24 hours, then should be scrubbed and left immersed in a container under a gently running tap for a further 24 hours. This will destroy any potential disease organisms or toxins that would otherwise be introduced to the aquarium.

Similar treatment should be applied to any bogwood used in the aquarium. Freshly cut material from living trees should never be used, as it could release harmful sap into the water. Deadwood collected from the seashore, from the banks of rivers, or from heathland will have been weathered. Such wood should be thoroughly scrubbed and washed before use. The best type of wood for use in the aquarium for decorative purposes is bogwood, which is almost fossilized and will have lain for many years under mud and water. Specialist firms dredge up such wood and prepare it for the pet market. Suitable pieces can usually be purchased inexpensively from your pet shop.

Aquatic Plants

Aquaculture can be described as a branch of horticulture pertaining to the successful cultivation of aquatic plants under controlled conditions. Plants in the aquarium not only contribute to the general esthetic appeal, they assist in the recycling of waste products from the animal inmates of the tank. During the process of photosynthesis they take in carbon dioxide and emit oxygen, thus helping to keep the water fresh and healthy. Organic excretory matter will also be filtered and absorbed through the root systems, which also will help stabilize the aquarium substrate. In addition, plants provide shelter for some of the tank's smaller dwellers and refuge for those being harassed by others. In some cases they provide sites on which certain amphibians will lay their eggs.

The addition of certain aquatic plants adds a nice degree of color and beauty to almost any amphibian's tank. Photo by B. Kahl.

Suitable plant species for use in the aquarium will be described later, but it is necessary here to mention a few salient points. It is almost a waste of time to try and grow plants in an aquarium containing large amphibians (amphiumas, hellbenders, large bullfrogs, for example) as these creatures will continually uproot your efforts. Even medium sized amphibians (axolotls and *Xenopus*, for example) can pose problems but are not altogether impossible. Most smaller aquatic newts can cohabit with growing aquatic plants with few problems. Indeed, water plants are almost essential for the satisfactory reproduction of *Triturus* species, for example.

If aquatic plants are to be grown successfully in the aquarium substrate, a certain amount of preparation is necessary. Ideally, only those species of plants that come from the same habitat as the amphibians being kept should be used. As this is not always possible, plants that require similar conditions to the animals should be used. For example, do not use plants from temperate areas in a tropical tank, and vice versa. Many plants are affected by the actual water conditions and, in some cases, can be more difficult subjects to maintain than the amphibians themselves. As a generalization, aquatic plants and animals from tropical rain forest areas require soft, slightly acid water (pH 5.5—6.5), while those from temperate limestone areas require hard, alkaline water (pH 7.5—8.5). Useful data on the maintenance of certain pH levels and hardnesses in aquarium water will be gleaned from a good book on tropical fish or on aquatic plants.

While some plant species may thrive in the aquarium gravel without additional substrate (they will be fertilized by the waste materials from the animals), greater success will be accomplished if special conditions are created for the plants. An ideal medium for most aquarium plant species is produced as follows: place a 1 cm (0.5 in) layer of unwashed river sand on the aquarium bottom and cover this with a mosaic of peat slabs about 2.5

This **very attractive group of aquatic plants was photographed by J. Elias.**

cm (1 in) thick (these should be weighted down and soaked underwater for at least two weeks before use or they will keep floating to the surface). The spaces between the peat slices (about 1 cm—0.5 in) are filled with sterilized garden loam. This is covered with a further 1 cm (0.5 in) of unwashed river sand and finally with the decorative layer of aquarium gravel, which should slope upward from front to back of the tank.

Before planting the tank, it is a good idea to sketch out a few ideas on paper to give you an insight into how the final layout will appear. In general, taller plants should be placed toward the rear of the display, the shorter ones in the middle ground. The foreground should

Even a tank with this many plants can be appealing, although slightly more laborious to care for. Photo by B. Kahl.

be left relatively free of plants to provide free swimming space for the animals. It is best to add a small amount of water—say to a depth of 5 cm (2 in)—to the tank before planting. This should be poured over a sheet of glass or a plate to prevent disturbance of the substrate. Your plants will usually be obtained from pet shops. Inspect plants carefully before use, removing dead or decaying foliage and watching out for potential predators, parasites, or other undesirable additions. It is usually necessary to weigh down plants initially, to prevent them from floating to the surface before they have rooted. Metal weights are undesirable, but ceramic or glass beads tied loosely to the base of the plants with nylon thread will be adequate. The plants can be pushed into the substrate using a special forked planting tool, taking care not to disturb the lower layers too much. As the roots of the plants develop, they will form a dense mat and stabilize the peat and loam layers. It would, of course, be advantageous to allow a good establishment of the plants before any amphibians are introduced.

THE AQUATERRARIUM

The simplest aquaterrarium can be constructed using an aquarium divided with a water-tight glass panel to a height roughly half that of the tank. One side of the glass panel (which can be cemented in with silicone sealant) is set up as you would an aquarium, while the other side is filled with gravel and landscaped. Rocks can be arranged on a gradient at the edge of the dividing panel to allow easy access and egress by the occupants. If the partition is say 15 cm (6 in) high, the substrate of gravel can be 2.5 cm (1 in) deep, thus allowing for 12.5 cm (5 in) of water depth. It is very advantageous to have a drainage hole or holes in the base of the land area so that it does not become too waterlogged and pose a possible health hazard to plants and animals. This land area should be half-filled with pebbles and coarse gravel, then with a mixture of sterilized garden loam, peat, and clean, coarse sand. A slab of grassy turf can be placed over this or you can use clumps of moss, mossy bark, leaf mold, etc., to

Here are two simple aquaterraria that can be used for most of your anuran pets.

landscape. For extra decoration and for help in maintaining humidity, a few potted plants can be sunk into the substrate.

A more natural looking aquaterrarium can be made by using a very large tank and building a "river bank" up from the rear. In such cases the whole of the aquarium tank becomes the pond and the back wall is built up with natural rocks and cement. Here you will be able to exercise your artistic talents, as there are many possibilities. Tree roots can appear to come out of the bank below water and special cavities of sizes to take various plant pots can be left between some of the rocks. A lush growth of plants in the bank area will be very attractive. If they are kept potted you can exchange them from time to time, giving those from the aquaterrarium a period of rest and recuperation.

Above the tank, you can install a wooden-framed glass window, which can be opened for access to the tank and the land area. A mesh-covered framework above this will provide ventilation. With care and dedication it is possible to produce an exhibit that is not only highly decorative and attractive, but ideal for many amphibious woodland species of amphibians that should breed readily, provided you supply the necessary seasonal conditions. One word of warning: when using cement in such a structure, ensure that

the lime has been completely dissolved out before introducing animals or plants. This is best done by filling the tank with water for 24 hours, then draining and scrubbing the surfaces. This should be repeated about four times.

THE TERRARIUM

The terrarium is one with little or no water area. It is suitable for several species of salamander that do not breed in water or for species of frog that require very small bodies of water (bromeliad breeders, for example). A glass-fronted wooden box can be used for such a terrarium, but because a high humidity will be required, it is best to use an all-glass tank. The shape of the tank will vary according to the type of animals to be kept. If you intend to keep tree frogs, for example, the container should preferably be taller than its width. For terrestrial inhabitants a shallow container with a greater floor area is preferred. Of course, there are no hard and fast rules, and you may wish to keep both arboreal and terrestrial species in the same tank.

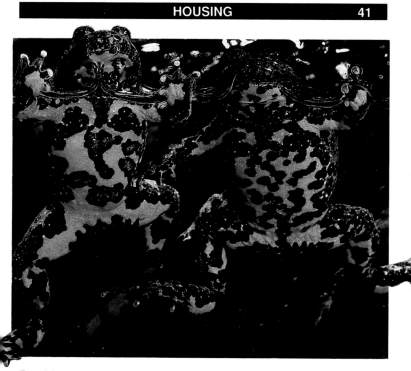

Bombina bombina, **the fire-bellied toad, is a popular pet in its native Europe. Photo by B. Kahl.**

As an example, a tank for a pair of small treefrogs need be no larger than 50 x 50 x 75 cm tall (20 x 20 x 30 in). The base can be given a layer of gravel that you can cover with slabs of moss. A dead tree branch covered with epiphytic plants can be used as a centerpiece. Bromeliads that hold water in their bracts are particularly useful, and some frogs will hide and even breed in these. In most forms of indoor terraria specific life support systems are required in addition to the basic tank and its decorations. Such systems include heating, cooling, lighting, humidity control, ventilation, and filtration, all of which deserve more detailed discussion.

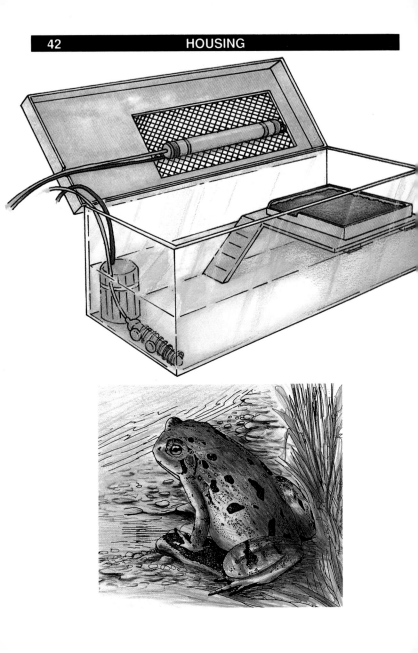

The Terrarium Lid

This is included here because the lid not only prevents your animals from escaping, it can be used to house some of the life support systems, especially lighting and heating, and it provides ventilation. A terrarium lid may be made from plastic, but it can also be made from exterior quality plywood that has been given a couple of coats of yacht varnish or non-toxic waterproof paint. A couple of large holes in the top of the lid can be covered with fine gauge mesh for ventilation. To allow for lighting and/or heating apparatus, the lid should be at least 15 cm (6 in) deep. To protect the animals, a mesh shield should be placed in the lid between the lighting and heating apparatus and the interior of the tank.

Heating

Most amphibians do not require basking temperatures as high as some reptile species. However, those from the tropics will require supplementary heating if kept in terraria in temperate to cold areas. Bear in mind that tropical species do not hibernate, so they will require warmth throughout the winter. Individual temperature requirements will be given in the species descriptions, but the choice of heating apparatus often rests with the individual.

One of the most convenient methods of heating is a simple thermostatically controlled aquarium heater. If you are keeping aquatic species in an aquarium, the heater is simply used in the same way it would be used for fish. However, an aquarium heater can also be used in an aquaterrarium and a terrarium to good effect. In the aquaterrarium it will not

Previous page: **Somewhat more complicated than the basic terrarium is this attractive 20-gallon setup. Many of the less demanding amphibs, like the *Bufo* shown on the left, can thrive in such an arrangement indefinitely.**

only heat the water but also the airspace by evaporation, at the same time maintaining high humidity. In the terrarium an aquarium heater can be placed in a container (a glass jar, for example) of water, where it will heat the air space and maintain humidity. Most aquarium heaters consist of an element situated in a heat-resistant waterproof glass tube. A thermostat can be present in the same tube or separate. This latter form of thermostat is useful in terraria, as it can be placed to better control air temperature. In other words, the thermostat is set at the temperature required and placed in the air space, while the heater is placed in a container of water. In combination with the lighting this should be sufficient to maintain water and air temperatures in a range of 23-30°C (73-86°F), which is satisfactory for many tropical species.

Other forms of heating include tungsten bulbs, which will give both light and heat. You can experiment with various wattages and a thermometer until a satisfactory temperature range is achieved. Infrared bulbs of the type that emit dry radiant heat are, in general, unsuitable for amphibians as they will have a desiccatory effect and it will be almost impossible to maintain humidity. Recently, a range of cable and pad heaters has become available. Cables may be placed under tanks, pads below the substrate inside the tank. These may also be operated by a thermostat. As amphibians are ectothermic (body temperature controlled by the surrounding environmental temperature), they maintain their preferred body temperature by moving from one temperature zone into another. It is therefore advisable to have a range of temperatures available in the terrarium. This can be accomplished by placing the heater at one end of the terrarium so the air temperature will be less at the other end. If we can maintain the range of 23-30°C (73-86°F) suggested above, most tropical species will be able to find a spot where they can enjoy their preferred temperature.

If aquarium heaters are used

Certain species, like this Cope's gray treefrog, *Hyla chrysocelis*, require moderate heat in order to be comfortable. Photo by R. T. Zappalorti.

as the sole form of heating and the thermostat is in the water, the water temperature will remain constant but the air temperature will be progressively diminished over the land area and can be further controlled by changes in ventilation. In most areas, there is a marked drop in temperature at night, so it is advisable to reduce the temperature in the terrarium each night by 6-8°C (10-12°F). In most cases this is accomplished simply by switching off the heater and allowing the terrarium to cool progressively to room temperature overnight. However, if the tank is situated in an unheated room or outbuilding in the winter, some form of supplementary night heating will be required. Aquarium tanks containing totally aquatic specimens do not normally require a nightly temperature reduction as these species are more accustomed to constant temperatures and very slow changes.

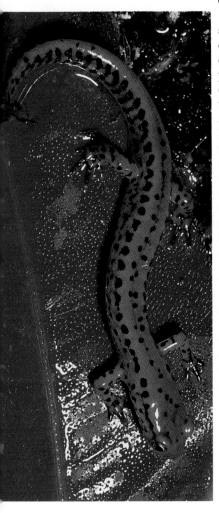

Cooling

Some readers may be surprised to find a section on cooling in this book. However, certain species of amphibians, particularly montane species, cannot be maintained for long if they are kept at temperatures above those of their native habitats. Other species may require temperature reductions at certain times of the year in order to maintain normal life cycles. Recently, the husbandry of cool area species has been given much attention and there is now no reason why such species cannot be kept successfully in home aquaria or terraria.

The simplest method of cooling a terrarium is to have a tank of water in a refrigerator with a flexible pipe rigged to a circulatory pump operated by a thermostat. The thermostat is set to switch on the pump and

Some species of salamander, such as this long-tail, *Eurycea longicauda,* may require an annual "cooling period" if expected to breed. Photo by R. T. Zappalorti.

pass cold water into the water area of the terrarium when the required maximum temperature is reached and to switch it off at the required minimum temperature.

Lighting

Although most amphibian species are nocturnal and secretive, this does not mean to say they are not light-oriented; they recognize the cycle of day and night. In subtropical and temperate latitudes, where hours of daylight (photoperiod) vary from season to season, amphibians are even more conscious of light cycles. The coming of spring is heralded by longer periods of daylight that bring amphibians out of hibernation, ready for the breeding season. In captivity, the light from a window may be adequate for our amphibians, but if we want to grow plants in the terrarium some form of supplementary lighting will be necessary. Additionally, good lighting of the terrarium adds to its esthetics and allows the observer a better view of the inhabitants.

For best results, and especially if breeding your

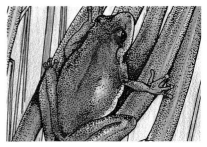

Most frogs, including this squirrel treefrog, *Hyla squirella*, need proper attention to light cycles (photoperiod) in order to thrive.

amphibians is contemplated, you should try and reproduce a light/dark cycle in the terrarium similar to that of the native habitat of the species in question. If you keep or intend to keep more than one species in the same terrarium, try to choose those which require similar light/dark cycles.

It is best not to allow your terrarium to be lit by natural sunlight as it is very easy for the sun to heat the terrarium interior to lethal levels in a very short time indeed. If plants are to flourish in the terrarium, a good quality artificial light will have to be used. Broad-spectrum fluorescent tubes that emit a quality of light ideal for plant growth and which, at the same time, will enhance the colors in your terrarium, are available from pet shops. There are various makes, sizes, and wattages, so it is advisable to get your dealer to demonstrate the qualities of some of these before you make a decision to purchase.

Ventilation

In the humid terrarium environment, good ventilation is essential to prevent a build-up of foul air, to discourage growth of unpleasant molds or bacterial growths in the substrate, and to remove excess carbon dioxide. However, the ventilation must be gentle, without creating excessive drafts. All terrarium lids should be adequately ventilated. The greater the vented area the better. A simple frame covered with fine plastic or metal gauze is ideal. More efficient ventilation can be achieved by having additional vent panels in the sides of the terrarium. If you have acrylic or plexiglass panels, these can be easily drilled with ventilation holes.

An aquarium aeration pump is ideal for further improving the ventilation. Various sizes of pump are available to suit different volumes of water. For a medium terrarium, a small diaphragm pump will usually be adequate. The pump is attached to a plastic tube running into the aquarium or water part of the terrarium and an air diffuser stone is attached to the end of the tube. When the pump is switched on, tiny bubbles of air are emitted through the stone and rise to the water surface. This will create gentle air movement in the terrarium. Your air pump will perform a number of other useful functions in the terrarium. The aeration of the water will help to keep it sweet and clean and will be essential if you are rearing gilled larvae. The bubbles will not only help oxygenate the water themselves, but they will cause water currents which will expose a greater volume of the water to the atmosphere and enhance gas exchange (dissolving of oxygen and dissipation of carbon dioxide). In addition, the bubbles will help maintain the air space temperature if the water is

If this little fellow, a mountain treefrog, *Hyla eximia*, is expected to thrive, it must be given a delicately balanced humidity level. Photo by R. D. Bartlett.

heated and they will also increase humidity. The air pump may also be used to create waterfalls or filters.

Care should be taken as to the source of air drawn into the pump. The atmosphere in the average home can be dangerous to your sensitive amphibians, with cooking fumes, fly sprays, deodorants, tobacco smoke, etc., being frequently released. It is best to have the inlet outside so that external air is drawn in. In the winter the inlet pipe may be passed near a radiator so that

Left: **Good filtration is essential, especially with totally aquatic species like this African clawed frog,** *Xenopus laevis.* **Photo by M. Gilroy.**

Opposite: **Tanks with much plant material, like the one shown here, require more filtration than tanks without plants. Photo by B. Kahl.**

the air is warmed before it enters the terrarium.

Filtration

Some amphibian inhabitants of your terraria, such as clawed frogs and axolotls are particularly "messy," and, unless you want to change the water frequently, a filter is essential. In fact, a filter in every terrarium is highly recommended, especially if successful rearing is contemplated. Unfiltered water tends to foul and become dirty quickly, causing unpleasant smells in the home and health hazards to the inmates. Various kinds of filter are available from pet shops, the simplest being box filters operated by an ordinary air pump on the principle that the rising bubbles drag the water through a filter medium, trapping the suspended solids. Such a filter is ideal and adequate for terraria with small volumes of water (up to 20 liters—4 gallons, for example), but the filter medium (often nylon wool) must be frequently renewed. Power filters are recommended

for larger volumes of water, and there are many types available; discuss the pros and cons with your dealer. Most filters are operated by a pump forcing water through various filter media. The filter should be used according to the manufacturer's instructions. The filter pump is usually strong enough for you to return the water back to the terrarium via a "waterfall," which can be attractively landscaped. Such a waterfall will help improve humidity in the air space.

Humidity

Most amphibians cannot abide dry conditions and will soon desiccate if humidity fails. We should aim to have a humidity in the terrarium air space of not less than 60%. Although an air filter or aerator can be used to enhance humidity, it may still be necessary to mist-spray parts of the terrarium once or twice per day, especially in areas with dry external climates or in centrally heated dwellings. The type of spray bottle used for indoor plants is ideal for this purpose.

Almost all amphibians, like this mole salamander, *Ambystoma talpoideum,* need a high moisture level. Photo by W. B. Allen, Jr.

OUTDOOR HOUSING FOR AMPHIBIANS

If you are keeping native amphibians or species heralding from a climate similar to your own, one very satisfactory method of accommodating them is in an outdoor enclosure. Of course, a simple garden pond may be all that is required to attract native species in your area, or

If you are going to house something like these canyon treefrogs (*Hyla arenicolor*) outdoors, be sure the area they are in is escape-proof. Photo by K. Lucas, Steinhart Aquarium.

you can introduce wild collected spawn or tadpoles, but if you want to have some control over what you keep, then the pond must be enclosed with a suitable wall. If you intend to keep treefrogs, then the whole area, including the roof, will have to be enclosed with shade cloth or something similar. Many terrestrial and aquatic species of frog and salamander will require a wall about 1.2 m (4 ft) high, which will prevent the more energetic individuals from jumping or climbing out. An overhang at the top of the wall will make it even more secure. The inside of the wall should be rendered as smoothly as possible. The enclosure can be attractively landscaped with rocks, plants, perhaps a waterfall and ponds at different levels, allowing a choice of breeding sites. For more information on the construction of garden ponds, waterfalls, and suitable plants, read some of the literature on water gardening.

General Management

FOODS AND FEEDING

Almost all amphibians are wholly carnivorous (meat-eating), though most of them live on a diet of insects and other small invertebrates, at least when they are in the adult stage. Larvae of many species, however, will feed on vegetable matter, especially in their early stages. An exception to the rule is members of the family Sirenidae, which feed on both vegetable and animal matter throughout their lives.

All animals, whether they are humans, giraffes, whales, sharks, goldfish, canaries, grasshoppers, frogs, or salamanders, require a balanced diet for their basic metabolism to function correctly. Such a diet must contain the correct proportions of proteins, carbohydrates, fats, vitamins, and minerals. Amphibians generally consume a wide range of insects, spiders, worms, and so on, while some of the larger species may take small vertebrates including fishes, birds,

mammals, reptiles, and other amphibians, as well as carrion. Most adult amphibians do not deliberately take vegetable matter, but a certain amount may be ingested during the capture of prey or in the undigested contents of the prey animal's gut. Wild amphibians obtain their balanced diet by feeding on a variety of organisms. Species that hibernate or estivate must see that they obtain enough food in favorable times in order to see them through their long periods of dormancy and prepare them for breeding when they emerge.

Most species will take livefoods only, relying on movement of the prey to stimulate a feeding response. Some aquatic species, however, can detect stationary or dead prey by the sense of smell or touch. It may be a great temptation to the home terrarium keeper to feed his animals solely on the most easily available food, such as mealworms, which can be conveniently and regularly

Some amphibs, like this pine barrens treefrog, *Hyla andersonii,* can live quite well on a simple diet of crickets and the occasional vitamin supplement. Photo by R. T. Zappalorti.

purchased. Although these insects are an excellent food and are taken readily by most medium to larger amphibians, there is evidence that they are lacking in certain important minerals, so they should be used only as one ingredient in a more varied diet.

COLLECTING LIVEFOODS

Perhaps the most useful means of providing your animals with a varied diet is to collect wild insects and other invertebrates. Not only will this relieve the monotony of cultured foodstuffs, it will most certainly introduce additional beneficial nutrients to the diet of your animals.

The best means of collecting a variety of terrestrial insects and spiders is to "sweep" through herbage with a canvas-reinforced sweep-net. You can make one of these with some strong wire (such as a heavy coat hanger), half a broomstick, and some net curtain material; canvas (or denim) is used around the mouth of the net to protect the material from wear and snagging. Commercially produced sweeping nets are

A few of the larger salamanders, like this tiger salamander *Ambystoma tigrinum*, get large enough to accept small mice. Photo by K. T. Nemuras.

available through many biological supply companies that sell supplies to high school and college biology departments. Their catalogs are always interesting to look through. The mouth of the net is simply swept through the foliage of trees, shrubs, and tall grass and the resulting catch is placed in glass or plastic containers for transport home. During the warmer months of the year, such sweepings will provide you with a great variety of beetles, flies, caterpillars,

Caterpillars are also perfectly acceptable to most amphibians. Photo by P. Freed.

grasshoppers, spiders, and so on. The collected invertebrates should be graded into suitable sizes and dangerous species (wasps, predatory true bugs, heavily armored beetles, etc.) removed. These various creatures will be eagerly taken by your amphibians. It is not advisable to introduce many insects at a time into the terrarium; allow one lot to be devoured before adding the next or you are likely to get escapees into the house; insects will also drown in the water and spoil, making it unhealthy for your amphibians.

A word of precaution is necessary here. Before you collect any insects or other wild

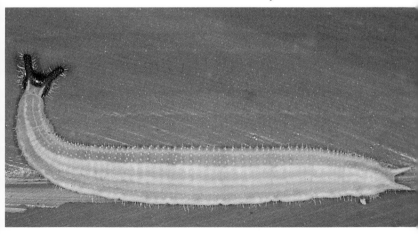

Mealworm beetles are a good meal, but are best supplemented by other foods. Photo by M. Gilroy.

foods, be sure that you are not collecting in an area that has been sprayed with insecticides or herbicides. Amphibians are very sensitive to even low residues of these chemicals. Often it is best to not collect within 25 meters of a roadside (because of herbicides as well as automobile pollutants adhering to vegetation) or within 100 meters of a field presently being used for a crop. There are so many dangerous chemicals present near man and his holdings that you may have to restrict your collecting to the vicinity of small parks and similar woodlots. If you are tempted to collect in a park, be sure to get permission from an official; many parks allow insect collecting, but others do not. If you live in Europe you may have to be aware of local and national endangered species laws protecting various species and categories of insects; the same may be true in a few spots in the United States known to contain endangered beetles and butterflies. Don't do anything illegal when attempting to collect anything anywhere.

Another method of collecting insects in bulk is the use of a flytrap. Several designs are available commercially or you may try making your own. This is easily done by using insect screening on a wire or wooden frame mounted on a flat board about 30 cm (1 ft) square. A 1 cm (0.5 in) hole is drilled in the center of the board and a plastic funnel is inverted over this, or you can use a cone with a hole in the top made from insect mesh. The board is placed on four bricks or wooden blocks so that there is adequate space beneath. A piece of rotten meat or fish is placed under the board and will attract flies to feed or lay eggs (the maggots that hatch

Maggots are also fine for feeding, but again should only be given in conjunction with something else. Photo by M. Gilroy.

from these are an additional supply of livefood!). When alarmed or after feeding, the flies will make for the strongest source of light, which is the hole in the board, directly above them. After making their way through the funnel they

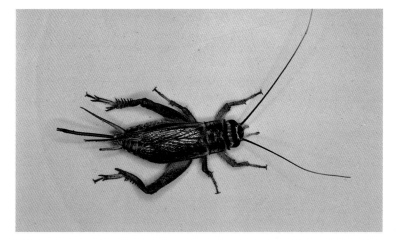

The house cricket is one of the most easily obtainable and nutritious of all food items. Photo by M. Gilroy.

will be trapped in the mesh cage. To remove flies, you can have a muslin "sleeve" set into one side of the cage and knot it when not in use. When you wish to collect flies you can undo this and insert your hand with a jar in which to scoop them up.

By turning over logs, rocks, and other ground debris, you will be sure to capture a variety of grubs, beetles, earthworms, pill bugs, slugs, and snails.

Many small insects congregate in flower heads; these are very suitable for small amphibian species and newly metamorphosed youngsters. They can be collected with a "pooter," which is a glass or plastic bottle with a cork or rubber stopper through which two glass tubes pass. One tube, the mouthpiece, is bent over at right angles and passes just through the cork; the other tube is straight but passes to near the bottom of the bottle. On its outer end a piece of flexible rubber tubing is attached. The end of this tubing is placed near the insects to be collected. When

A bowlful of fresh *Daphnia*. Photo by C. O. Masters.

you suck sharply on the mouthpiece, the insects will be drawn through the glass tube into the bottle. To prevent accidental inhalation of insects, a piece of cotton or cheesecloth wadding should be placed in the mouthpiece.

A good food source for very small terrestrial amphibians is aphids (commonly called greenflies or blackflies). These often appear in large numbers on the growing tips of many plants. It is a simple matter to cut off a tip, complete with its ration of aphids, and place it in the terrarium.

Ants and termites can often be collected in large numbers. Although ants are rejected by most amphibian species (probably due to their acid taste) there are a few species which specialize in eating ants. Many toads and narrow-mouthed frogs will take large numbers of ants. Termites (white ants) are taken eagerly by most species and are a particularly nutritious item. If you have access to termite nests, you can simply chip a piece of the mound away at regular intervals and place it complete with the insects in the terrarium. The remaining termites will quickly repair the nest and you can collect specimens time after time.

Water-dwelling amphibians and carnivorous larvae will require aquatic livefoods. Various freshwater crustaceans, ranging from the tiny copepods such as *Cyclops* and waterfleas such as *Daphnia* to the relatively large freshwater shrimps and crayfish can be netted or found by turning over rocks near the edges of streams, creeks, etc. The larvae of many flying insects (mosquitoes, mayflies, etc.) are aquatic and are also excellent food. When collecting aquatic livefoods, be careful not to introduce voracious larvae, such as those of dragonflies and carnivorous water beetles, which could make short work of your amphibians.

Termites may not be easy to come by, but they can still be utilized as a food source. Photo by G. Dingerkus.

CULTURED LIVEFOODS

For one reason or another it will not always be possible to provide your amphibians with collected wild livefoods all the time. Maybe you are short of time for collecting (especially if

Left: **This photo shows a variety of live foods. From top: black worms, tubifex, and brine shrimp. Photo by I. Francais.**

Opposite: **Mealworms are commonly sold in pet stores, but are not a complete diet. Photo by M. Gilroy.**

you live in the city and would have to travel out into the country) or there may be an actual shortage of wild livefoods (as in the winter months of cooler areas—if you are hibernating your amphibians, of course, there will be no problem). It is therefore always beneficial to have a stand-by supply of cultured livefoods. Today there are many suppliers of various livefoods. If you don't want to go to the trouble of breeding your own mealworms or crickets, for example, you can simply collect or purchase a regular small supply of insects. Some producers are glad to supply insects regularly by mail order. However, many hobbyists choose to culture their own livefood after having purchased the initial stock. A brief guide to the more usual cultured livefoods follows.

Mealworms

These well-known grubs are the larvae of the flour beetle, *Tenebrio molitor*, and are probably the oldest commercially produced livefood for pet animals. They may be purchased from dealers in any quantity and are relatively easy to propagate. Allow a few of the mealworms to pupate and metamorphose into adult beetles that are brown and about 8 mm, 0.4 in, long. These should be placed in a container with a close-fitting but ventilated (gauze) lid, along with a 5 cm (2 in) layer of food mixture (bran and crushed oats is ideal). Place a piece of sacking or absorbent cloth over the food mixture and put a couple of pieces of carrot or a similar vegetable on top to provide moisture. The beetles will soon mate and lay eggs in the medium. In about seven days the eggs hatch into tiny mealworms that grow steadily, reaching full size in about 15 weeks. If you start a new culture each month and dispose of the oldest one (keeping about four going), a regular supply of mealworms of all sizes will be available. For the best results, cultures should be kept at temperatures of 25-30°C (77-86°F).

Crickets

Cultured crickets have become a very popular livefood for many insectivorous pets in recent times. They are easy to breed and very nutritious for your amphibians. There are several species available, but the most commonly encountered are domestic species of the genus *Gryllus*. Cricket cultures can be obtained from cricket farms. They come in various sizes from 3 to 25 mm (0.15 in to 1 in) depending on what stage of the life cycle they are in. This means that there is a cricket the size to suit most sizes of amphibian. Crickets are fairly easy to breed in a ventilated plastic box kept at a temperature of about 25°C (77°F). Feed them on a mixture of bran and crushed oats, plus a little green food or raw root vegetable. A dish containing a piece of water-soaked cotton wadding will double as a drinking fountain and a medium in which the insects can lay their eggs. The eggs will hatch in about 20 days. The young can be reared to various sizes on the same diet as the adults.

Cockroaches

These are common in many places, especially in inner cities. They are a versatile form of livefood for amphibians. Several species will breed if given conditions similar to those for crickets described above. The tiny first instar nymphs make excellent food for smaller amphibians and newly metamorphosed youngsters. However, be sure they do not escape into your house and become pests. Additionally, because of the number of roach poisons being used today, some very slow in their action, any stock of wild roaches may be chemically contaminated even though healthy in appearance.

Grasshoppers and Locusts

Good food value and larger than crickets, grasshoppers and locusts are somewhat more difficult to breed. Perhaps it is wise to just buy a few occasionally as a treat for your larger pets.

Flies

There are many thousands of fly species, and most of these are ideal food for amphibians. Fruitflies, *Drosophila*, have long

Contrary to popular opinion, it is not at all difficult to breed crickets yourself. Photo by M. Gilroy.

been used as experimental insects in laboratories. Due to the speed with which they reproduce, these little flies, about 2.5 mm (0.1 in) in length have been found to be ideal for research into genetics. Consequently their breeding has been taken to a fine art. Even "wingless" (vestigial-winged) specimens are bred in large numbers. These are very useful for feeding to small amphibians as you do not then have the problem of flies escaping to all corners of the house. Fruitfly cultures and instructions on how to proliferate them may be obtained from college biology laboratories, biological supply houses, some pet shops, and even by mail order. Quantities of wild fruitflies can soon be collected if you place a box of banana skins or some rotten fruit in a remote corner of the garden. During the warmer

Fruitflies can also be easily cultured and are good for some of the smaller species of amphibian. Photo by M. Gilroy.

parts of the year this will be teeming with fruitflies in no time at all, and they can be simply collected with a fine-mesh net.

House flies, *Musca*, and lesser house flies, *Fannia*, are also suitable for small to medium sized amphibians, while the larger greenbottles, *Lucilia*, and bluebottles, *Calliphora*, are suitable for your larger pets. Most of these can be caught in a flytrap in the summer. A more convenient way of getting flies

is to purchase maggots from a bait shop. The maggots themselves make a reasonable food for larger amphibians, but do not use them in great numbers as they have a very tough skin and are hard for your pets to digest; just one or two occasionally is adequate. It is best to keep the maggots in containers of clean bran or sawdust and allow them to pupate. In a few days the adult flies will emerge. If you place a few pupae in a small plastic lunch box with a fly-sized hole in the lid, the flies will escape singly and the whole box can be placed in the terrarium. Many amphibians, especially toads, will soon learn the location of this food source and will patiently wait near the box for flies to emerge.

Earthworms

Earthworms and brandlings are often available from bait suppliers and can be collected in the garden or elsewhere. They are excellent food for larger amphibians or can be chopped into pieces for smaller ones. As pieces of earthworm continue to wriggle for some time after being chopped, they are accepted readily by many species. You can ensure a regular supply of earthworms by placing a pile of damp, dead leaves in a shady corner and covering it with a piece of sacking. If you spray the sacking with water regularly, earthworms will soon congregate among the decaying leaves, from which you can collect them at perhaps weekly intervals. As one supply becomes exhausted, you can start again in another spot.

If you are feeding your pets worms regularly, be sure to stock up during the cold winter months. Photo by M. Gilroy.

Tubifex

These small red aquatic worms are often available from pet shops. They are a nutritious food and especially suitable for small aquatic frogs, salamanders, newts, and advanced larvae. Be sure that you only purchase fresh worms, not clumps of dead grayish specimens that may poison your pets. Wash the clump thoroughly for at least a half hour before feeding (leave the cup or bag of worms under the slow drip of a coldwater faucet) and store them in fresh water in the refrigerator. Though tubifex are an excellent food, they present a problem of

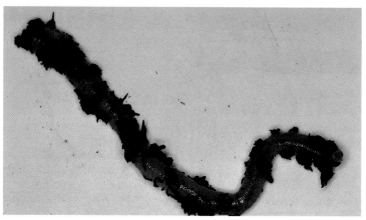

Whiteworms are a very good conditioning food for breeding pairs of smaller amphibians. Photo by B. Degen.

contamination from sewage and heavy metals, thus the precautions.

Whiteworms

Cultures of these tiny worms, *Enchytraeus* can be purchased complete with instructions on propagation. They are a useful food for newly metamorphosed frogs and newts and for very small salamander species. Cultures are available at most pet shops and by mail order. Any basic book on keeping tropical fishes probably will have instructions for culturing the little worms. They often are used to feed fish fry. Their major drawback is that cultures often become overgrown with a bacterial culture that smells bad and looks worse. Well worth the trouble of keeping up, however.

FOOD SUPPLEMENTS

In general, animals that receive a wide selection of livefoods are unlikely to suffer mineral or vitamin deficiencies. However, when a variety of insects is in short supply (such as during the winter when we have to make do with cultured foods such as mealworms or crickets over long periods) it is advisable to give a regular vitamin and mineral supplement perhaps two or three times per week. Suitable preparations may be obtained in fluid, powder, or tablet form from pet shops and veterinarians. Powders are probably the most suitable as they can be dusted directly onto the livefood. The insects are placed in a small container, moistened a bit, and the powder is dusted over them. A gentle shake will ensure each insect has a film of powder over its surface; the insects are then given to your pets in the normal manner.

PREPARED FOODS

Axolotls, clawed frogs, and other aquatic amphibians will take strips of meat or fish, and some may even take trout pellets or other manufactured foods. Do not feed fatty meat or fish; provide as lean a piece as possible; don't use saltwater fish as a food. Never feed more than the amphibians can eat in one go. A little and often is better than too much at once, otherwise old food will pollute the water.

FEEDING METHODS

Most amphibians can be fed every other day; more often may lead to refusal to feed. Feed only as much as will be taken in a few minutes. The correct amounts of food will have to be ascertained by experimentation. Most terrestrial species are initially attracted to their prey by its movement, so in most cases it is pointless giving dead food. However, some of the larger terrestrial salamanders may be trained to take small pieces of meat by placing it in front of them and jiggling it with a very fine broom straw.

Health and Hygiene

Confined in relatively small areas, as in the terrarium, the importance of hygiene for the good health of our amphibians cannot be underestimated. Hygiene is the science of prevention of disease. By this we are not necessarily talking about soap and disinfectants. Cleanliness, of course, is a very important aspect of hygiene, but so is providing your terrarium inmates with optimum conditions for a life of contentment, devoid of stress. Stress in itself can be a factor that reduces an animal's normal resistance to disease, so we must ensure that the accommodations we provide for our amphibians are as comfortable as possible.

In general, most amphibians do not adapt well to surroundings that are alien to them. Just imagine what happens when we remove a frog from a cool, peaty, grassy meadow, or a salamander from dank, mossy woodland and place either in a tank containing chlorinated tap water at room temperature in your house and leave the lights on until midnight. Common sense will tell you that this is just the thing to cause stress.

Light intensity, photoperiod, and temperature should be similar to that found in the amphibian's original habitat. Excessive chlorine, as well as excessive hardness, in some domestic water supplies can be dangerous to your animals' health. Always use soft water where possible. If you can collect rainwater this is ideal (but today it might be safest to run a few tests on acidity and possible chemical contamination first). Alternatively, leave tap water to stand for at least 24 hours to allow free chlorine to disperse before it is used. It is not recommended that de-chlorination chemicals be used, as there is no evidence

Budgett's frog, *Lepidobatrachus laevis*, is, like other frogs, exceptionally sensitive to unclean surroundings. Photo by R. D. Bartlett.

that these are not harmful to the sensitive skins of amphibians.

SELECTION OF SPECIMENS

One important aspect of hygiene is to ensure that your new animals are free of disease from the word go. This is especially important when you are introducing new specimens to existing stock. Wild-collected amphibians are almost always healthy; those that had been ill would have been quickly eaten by predators. However, capture and confinement can induce stress, so try and make this as humane as possible!

If buying your amphibians from a pet shop, first impressions of the shop itself can be important. The means by which animals are commercially trapped, transported, and confined for wholesale and retail sale can be extremely stressful. Recent legislation in many countries has been designed to ensure that wild-caught animals, even "lowly" ones, get the best treatment possible, but unfortunately there still seems to be a certain amount of illegal activity in animal trading. If the premises are dirty, untidy, and smelly, with overcrowded tanks, turn your back quickly and go elsewhere. You will often see dead specimens mixed up with the live ones in such premises. Good pet shop management is concerned with the welfare of

every animal in their possession and will ensure that all are kept and displayed in the cleanest and most hygienic of conditions.

Before purchasing any specimen, it should be carefully examined. Select only those animals that are plump and have an unblemished skin. The eyes should be open and bright, with correctly shaped pupils. Avoid specimens with sunken abdomens and exaggeration of the bones in the pelvic area (unless natural, as in some frogs); this is a sign of starvation, often brought on by some other disease. Specimens with injuries, sores, or cysts in the skin should be discarded. Look for traces of fungus infection or red leg. Avoid specimens with obvious eye disorders. Specimens should be wary of the hand and should attempt to hop or run away when touched. Do not accept specimens that show no fright, flight, or fight.

HANDLING

In the strict sense of the word, amphibians are not "pets" to be picked up and fondled. Most amphibians

A handful of young marsupial frogs, *Gastrotheca riobambae*. Photo by M. Auber-Thomay and F. Letellier, courtesy of Dr. D Terver, Nancy Aquarium, France.

dislike being handled, and a warm, sweaty hand is not only uncomfortable to a frog or salamander, but the salt content of the sweat can be dangerous to it if you hold the delicate little creature for too long. Amphibians should be handled as infrequently as possible and then only for examination purposes. Many amphibians unaccustomed to being handled will release the fluid contents of the cloaca on being picked up. This is the

Most amphibians are very delicate and should only be handled when absolutely necessary. Photo of a male crested newt, *Triturus cristatus*, by M. Gilroy.

animal's reserve supply of body fluid and must be replaced. Ensure that an amphibian that has discharged its reserves has access to water as soon as possible. Amphibians seldom drink in the normal sense but absorb water through the skin.

A time when it will be essential to handle an amphibian is when you are contemplating its purchase. Be sure to wash the hands before handling and rinse them well in clear water, leaving them wet. A small frog or salamander can be gently cupped in the hands and examined by spreading the fingers. Larger, robust frogs should be gripped gently but firmly around the waist with their powerful hind legs stretched out to prevent them from kicking. Aquatic amphibians and tadpoles can be caught in a net made from soft material and examined without any need for handling, other than moving the net material away from the body.

Bear in mind that many amphibians have powerful protective poisons that they release from glands in the skin. Some of these can be extremely dangerous if you get them in your eyes or mucous membranes. Therefore, always wash your hands thoroughly after handling amphibians. Some species are also unable to tolerate the poisons of others, so don't keep more than one species in a terrarium or aquarium unless you are absolutely sure they are tolerant of each other.

TRANSPORT

Capture and transport are probably the most stressful times for amphibians, so it is important that we make this process as easy as possible for them. Terrestrial species can be transported in plastic boxes with a number of holes drilled in the lid for ventilation purposes. To keep the animals moist and to prevent them from being injured if the boxes are dropped or roughly handled, the boxes may be loosely packed with sphagnum moss. Do not use foam PVC or rubber unless you are sure it is inert; the author once lost a valuable consignment of newly metamorphosed *Ceratophrys ornata* that were poisoned by the exudate from PVC foam. Printers' ink can also be dangerous to amphibians, so never use newspaper. The animals should be transported as quickly as possible to their destination via the shortest possible route. Transport boxes should never be left exposed to the sun's rays or left in a parked car in sunny weather. Conversely, tropical species must have some protection from chilling during cold weather. In such cases it is wise to pack the transport boxes in some kind of an insulated container (a styrofoam box for example).

QUARANTINE

All amphibians being introduced to existing stock must first undergo a period of quarantine to ensure that they are not sick from some infectious disease that could be dangerous to all of your animals. Prepare a simple terrarium (or aquarium or

The popular Argentine horned frog, *Ceratophrys ornata*, takes well to captivity but does not like being moved about too much. Photo by G. Dingerkus.

aquaterrarium if appropriate) with the minimum of decorations but with the usual life-support systems and hiding places. This should preferably be kept in a

Even amphibs that look as healthy as this green toad, *Bufo viridis,* should be quarantined when first brought into the home. Photo by K. Lucas, Steinhart Aquarium.

separate room from the main stock. Install your new animals in this quarantine terrarium and observe them carefully over the next 21 days. If, after the prescribed period, the animals are still fit and healthy, then it should be safe to introduce them to your other animals.

GENERAL HYGIENE

The hot, humid environments required by tropical species in particular are, unfortunately, also ideal conditions in which fungi, bacteria, etc., can grow. If we use sterile materials when setting up, and if we get the right balance between ventilation and humidity, then we will reduce the danger of bacterial proliferation to a minimum.

Always wash the hands before and between each terrarium servicing even if there is no obvious sign of disease, thus ensuring that you are not the culprit spreading an epidemic among your charges. Terraria should be routinely cleaned out at regular intervals. It normally is necessary only to scrub the terrarium and its furnishings with clean water and to rinse it well. However, if you have had an outbreak of disease in a particular terrarium, isolate the sick animal(s) in a hospital terrarium in a separate room. Strip the terrarium and destroy plants, logs, etc., by burning. Rocks, gravel, and similar items can be discarded, or sterilized by boiling. The terrarium should be scrubbed out with a 10% solution of household bleach or with a veterinary povidone-iodine preparation, then thoroughly rinsed out several times with clean water.

HIBERNATION

Amphibians from subtropical, montane, or temperate climates usually hibernate during the colder parts of the year. They bury themselves in mud at the bottom of ponds or in deep terrestrial burrows, where they are safe from the frost. During hibernation, the basic metabolism is reduced dramatically and the animal is in a torpor and requires hardly any oxygen, let alone food. Although hibernating species can be kept "awake" all year around in captivity, there is evidence to suggest this will reduce their life expectancy and also render them unlikely to breed. It is the period of hibernation and the slow warming, coupled with the extended photoperiod in the spring, that bring such amphibians into breeding condition.

In captivity, however, a period of simulated hibernation is all our specimens require to give them an almost "normal" lifestyle including increased prospects of successful captive breeding. This can be accomplished by gradually decreasing the temperature and photoperiod in the terrarium over a period of about 14 days. Stop feeding the frogs and remove the terrarium to a frost-free outbuilding where the temperature can be maintained at not less than 4°C (39°F) and preferably not higher than 10°C (50°F). An alternative method is to place the frogs in slightly damp moss in a plastic container and to keep them in the refrigerator at about 4-5°C for a period of two

Before breeding can begin, almost all amphibians must first be hibernated. Photo of *Rana sylvatica* in amplexus by R. T. Zappalorti.

to three months. When the simulated hibernation period is to end, the reverse procedure should be carried out so that temperature and photoperiod are gradually increased.

ESTIVATION

Amphibians from areas likely to be arid for much of the year will estivate in the dry season and will emerge to breed in the rainy season. It is very difficult to give such animals optimum conditions in captivity, and it is therefore best to keep these species active by keeping them at least moist. A breeding response

Any and all ticks, like the one attached to the parotid gland of this marine toad, *Bufo marinus*, should be removed immediately. Photo by R. T. Zappalorti.

may then be triggered by suddenly increasing the amount of available water.

DISEASES AND TREATMENT

Most amphibians are remarkably resistant to disease if kept in optimum conditions, and most cases of ill health can usually be blamed on some inadequacy in the care. Veterinary science with regard to amphibian diseases is still in its infancy and, unfortunately, cures for diseases are often "hit and miss" affairs in which the medicine may be worse for the animal than the disease itself. However, there are a few veterinarians who devote themselves to the study of the more unusual types of pets, including amphibians. Your local veterinarian may be able to communicate with one or more of these experts if he is unsure himself. Some of the more common afflictions include the following.

Nutritional Deficiencies

Usually caused by a lack of certain minerals or vitamins in the diet, deficiencies are most common among amphibians fed on a monotonous diet of, for instance, mealworms and nothing else. It is very important to provide your animals with as great a variety of foodstuffs as possible. A routine application of a powdered multivitamin and mineral supplement in the food will prevent such deficiencies.

Mechanical Wounds

Open wounds or injuries to the skin are caused when frogs panic and attempt to escape. This usually occurs among newly captured specimens, which should be left in peace until they are accustomed to their new surroundings, after which such injuries will be less likely. Wounds are subject to bacterial infections that are potentially lethal, so treatment

Although treefrogs seem less susceptible to many ailments than do some other frogs, they should still be checked regularly. Photo of *Hyla arborea* by H. Heusser.

with an antibiotic may be necessary. Obtain advice from your veterinarian before applying any antiseptic preparations (some antiseptics that are quite safe for humans are lethal to amphibians).

Redleg

This is the most infamous disease of captive frogs and can also occur in salamanders. It is caused by the parasite *Aeromonas hydrophila.* Symptoms include the reddening of the skin (especially on the belly and the underside of the thighs), lethargy, and apathy. Sick animals should be immediately isolated. If caught in its early stages, redleg may be treated by immersing the infected animal in a 2% solution of copper sulfate or potassium permanganate. The use of an antibiotic such as tetracycline may also help. Consult a veterinarian for advice about this lethal disease.

Spring Disease

This is a lethal disease that occurs among certain temperate species in the breeding season. It is caused by *Bacterium ranicida.* Symptoms include a discoloration of the skin, lethargy, and a continuous "yawning." At present there seems to be no reliable treatment for this disease, though experimentation with antibiotics may be worth a try. Consult your veterinarian.

Fungal Infections

These may be particularly troublesome in aquatic amphibians and in tadpoles. The disease is seen as areas of inflamed skin surrounded by whitish tissue. Untreated, these infections can prove fatal. If caught in its early stages, a fungal infection can be treated by immersing the animal in a 2% solution of malachite green or Mercurochrome for five minutes, repeating after 24 hours if symptoms do not improve. If no improvement shows after three such treatments, a veterinarian should be consulted.

Above: An attractive southern toad, *Bufo terrestris*. Photo by P. A. Vargas.

Left: The spotted salamander, *Ambystoma maculatum*, is a very hardy species that will live long if properly cared for. Photo by B. Kahl.

Breeding

Each individual species has its own unique breeding habits, but a brief general summary of the captive breeding of amphibians will not go amiss. Most species require external stimuli to bring them into breeding condition. Temperate species, for example, usually breed in the spring, shortly after hibernation, and are affected by increases in temperature, photoperiod, and intensity of light. Tropical species may be influenced by changes in humidity, either seasonal or coincidental. At this stage it is thought prudent to divide our discussion on breeding, dealing first with anurans (frogs and toads), then with caudates (salamanders and newts), and finally with the caecilians.

FROGS AND TOADS

Some anurans can be persuaded to breed in captivity by injecting them with certain hormones. *Xenopus*, for example, is regularly bred in laboratories after being injected with HCG (human chorionic gonadotrophin), a hormone that is produced by pregnant women. In fact, *Xenopus* was once used in human pregnancy tests before more convenient methods were discovered. Needless to say, if you contemplate using hormone injections to induce your amphibians to breed, this should be done in conjunction with a veterinarian or licensed animal technician.

With most species, the sexes should be kept separately until a breeding response is required. Hormone-treated *Xenopus* will go into amplexus (a mating position in which the male grasps the female around the rear of the body and holds on) almost as soon as the pairs are introduced. This will last for about 48 hours. It is best to place breeding *Xenopus* into a spawning tank containing little other than the water, a heater, an aerator, and a filter (be sure the inlet to any filter is covered with fine mesh to prevent eggs or larvae from being sucked

This male Houston toad, *Bufo houstonensis*, is calling to attract a mate. Photo by P. Freed.

up). The eggs will fall to the bottom of the tank as they are being laid. A plastic grid placed on stones just above the tank bottom will allow the eggs to fall through and be protected from being eaten by the adults. After spawning, the adults can be moved back to their permanent tanks and the spawning tank can also be used as a rearing tank. The best temperature for hatching and rearing is 18-22°C (65-72°F), but the eggs will tolerate temperatures as low as 15°C (59°F) or as high as 25°C (77°F).

Dead eggs (which go opaque white) and/or larvae should be removed with a pipette as soon as they are seen. For the first 72 hours after hatching the tadpoles will not require feeding as they will be absorbing the contents of the yolk sac. As soon as they start to actively swim, they will feed. Grass or nettle powder may be used as a basic food; to this is added very small amounts (about 5% each) of powdered dried yeast, powdered egg, and a vitamin/mineral preparation. These ingredients are thoroughly mixed together and

water is added to make a paste. A quarter-teaspoon added to the rearing tank daily is adequate at first, this amount being increased slightly every few days as the larvae grow. As soon as the limbs are fairly well developed, start feeding the metamorphosing larvae on mosquito larvae, copepods, waterfleas, and chopped tubifex or whiteworms (do not over feed with the chopped food).

Seasonal breeders that spawn in large bodies of water can be treated similar to *Xenopus* in the early stages. Water temperature will, of course, depend on the native habitat of the species in question. For temperate species, pairs are introduced in the spring, after you have begun to gradually increase the temperature and photoperiod. These increases should continue until a maximum of 20°C (68°F) and a 15-hour period of "daylight" have been reached. Amphibious species that live on land after metamorphosis should be given facilities to leave the water as soon as they

A pair of African clawed frogs, *Xenopus laevis*, during the breeding process. Photo by R. Zukal.

are ready. This can be done by rearing them in an aquaterrarium with a sloping "bank." Alternatively, they may be reared in shallow water in which large flat stones are placed so that they just break the water surface.

When breeding amphibians that produce great numbers of offspring, it may be necessary to cull some of the larvae in order to prevent overcrowding. As the larvae grow, weed out the smaller specimens and dispose of them—native specimens can sometimes be released into the pond from which their parents came. Never release exotic specimens, which could be a future ecological hazard. It is much better to rear a small number of fit, healthy specimens than to have numerous weaklings.

As an example, let us look at the natural life cycle of a familiar ranid frog in more detail. This will give us an insight into the conditions required for them to breed successfully in captivity.

These tadpoles of a marsupial frog, *Gastrotheca riobambae*, already show the adult color pattern. Photo by M. Auber-Thomay and F. Letellier, courtesy Dr. D. Terver, Nancy Aquarium, France.

LIFE HISTORY OF THE EUROPEAN GRASS FROG

Once called the common frog, *Rana temporaria* is by no means common any more, especially in England. The author considers that the translation of the German name "grasfrosch" (grass frog) is thus now a more appropriate English name for it. The French name for the frog, "grenouille rousse" (red frog) is considered less desirable as, although occasional reddish specimens occur, they are more likely to be brownish or olive in color. A more complete description of appearance and natural range is given later. Here we are concerned with its breeding habits.

As if awakened from their winter sleep by an alarm bell, male grass frogs congregate in suitable ponds or other bodies of water in early spring. It is probably a certain length of photoperiod coupled with a suitably warm temperature that actually brings a male into readiness for mating. Although not the most vocal of frogs by far, the grass frog emits a quiet croak that comes in two pitches, one used to repel other, over-amorous males, the other to attract females, which arrive at the water somewhat later. Males often outnumber their partners by three or four to one, and there usually is considerable jostling among the suitors in trying to gain the

A breeding pair of *Rana temporaria*. Photo by B. Kahl.

attentions of a suitable mate.

Eventually each female finds a mate, though many males, usually the younger and/or the weaker ones, will be left out. The successful male grasps his chosen one around the body with his forelimbs just behind her forelimbs in a characteristic embrace known as amplexus. The grip is very strong and is aided by roughened areas of dark skin, known as nuptial pads, on his thumbs. These nuptial pads are only apparent at breeding time and will fade away for the remainder of the year. The embrace helps stimulate the female into laying her eggs, which may number up to 2000. The male is in the ideal position to fertilize the eggs, and as they emerge from the female's vent he showers them with a stream of sperm (milt).

The eggs are deposited in clumps of 100 or more, each individual egg being globular, black, and about 2-3 mm (0.1 in) in diameter. As soon as the eggs are free of the female's body and have been fertilized, the transparent gel surrounding them absorbs large amounts of water, forming a transparent, jelly-like protective capsule about 8 mm (0.35 in) in diameter. Having deposited the eggs, the parent frogs separate and show no further interest in them. Males may remain near the water to mate again, but eventually both parents will leave the water and spend the rest of the summer hunting insects in the damp grassy meadows.

The eggs hatch in four to five days, but the larvae (tadpoles) stay largely immobile and attached to the jelly mass for a day or two while they derive nourishment from the remainder of the yolk-sac to which they are still attached. Soon they take on the well-known tadpole form—large head, flat-finned tail, small gills, a pair of tiny eyes, and a horny pair of jaws within a broad disk with rows of tiny teeth used for rasping food. In the initial stages they feed on algae and debris that they rasp from the surfaces of plants and other objects. Their appetite increases with time, and soon they start to take animal matter ranging from tiny invertebrates to carrion. (One

This unusual shot shows a cluster of hatching northern leopard frogs, *Rana pipiens*. Photo by R. T. Zappalorti.

method of catching large numbers of tadpoles is to suspend a piece of meat tied to a string into a suitable water near the surface—the tadpoles congregating around the meat can be easily netted.)

When the body of the tadpole is some 10 mm (0.45 in) in length the hind limbs appear, followed by the forelimbs a few days later (in the larvae of salamanders, the forelimbs appear first). The transforming froglet derives some nourishment from its tail, which is absorbed into the body as the froglet develops. The gills are lost and the lungs develop, so the froglet must begin to take atmospheric air. It spends much time near the water's edge or suspended by its front

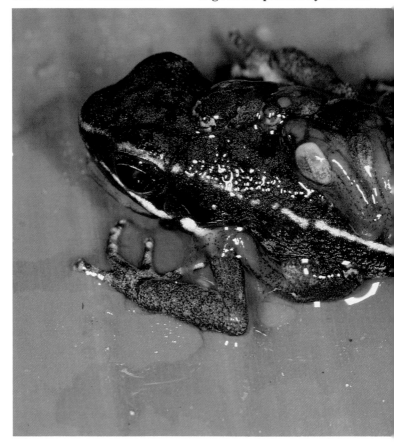

feet on a floating object such as a leaf. If conditions are dry, it remains in close proximity to the water, but a summer shower or a few heavy dews will see the little froglets leaving their ponds in great numbers (perhaps the origin of past "frog plagues" or "frogs rains") to creep into the protection of the lush summer vegetation. Except when breeding and hibernation, the European grass frog spends most of its time on land, but never too far from water.

SOME VARIATIONS

Most ranid species have a life history very similar to the "typical" one of the European grass frog just described. Bufonid toads also have similar life cycles, though eggs may be joined with jelly in chains or strings and wound around aquatic plants, rather than deposited in clumps. Many other species have a more or less "typical" life cycle of the type well known to us. However, there are also some highly variable reproductive methods and life styles, some of which can be described as astonishing. Frogs are more cosmopolitan than most

This poison arrow frog, *Dendrobates pictus*, is carrying its tadpoles on its back. Photo by P. Freed.

salamanders and have radiated into some amazingly diverse habitats, ranging from the tops of tropical rainforest trees to arid deserts and from the edge of the Arctic Circle to the peaks of mountains. The method of reproduction is often dictated by the habitat. Some tree-dwelling species, for example, may raise a family in a tiny water-filled hollow in a dead branch or in the water reservoir of a bromeliad. Others may build "foam nests" in or out of the water. Such foam nests are the result of froth released by females as they lay their eggs; the froth is beaten with the rear limbs until a foamy protective mass surrounds the eggs. Foam nests are often made in foliage overhanging water and, on hatching, the tadpoles wriggle out of the foam and drop into the water. Others make the foam nest on the water surface, often attached to aquatic plants or debris. The white foam makes the eggs invisible or perhaps distasteful to potential predators.

Although most species show no further interest in their offspring once eggs have been laid and fertilized, parental care is developed to varying degrees in some species to the extent that they may transport eggs or tadpoles around on their backs. With the European midwife toad, *Alytes obstetricans*, for example, the male winds a string of eggs around his back and hind limbs and carries them about until they are ready to hatch— he then deposits them in a suitably safe body of water where they continue to develop independently. The males of the colorful little tropical American dendrobatid frogs transport tadpoles around on their backs before depositing them in a suitable "nursery." The Surinam toad rears her young in pits on her back, while marsupial frogs rear theirs in a pouch on the female's back. Perhaps the most amazing method of all, however, is that performed by the gastric brooding frog, *Rheobatrachus silus*. Only discovered in 1973 in a small area of rainforest in southeastern Queensland, Australia, the female of this species swallows its newly hatched tadpoles, which

Note the egg string wrapped around the base of this male frog's hind legs. It is called the "midwife toad," *Alytes obstetricans*. Photo by H. Heusser.

develop to full metamorphosis in the mother's stomach. The fact that gastric juice inhibitors play an important part in this phenomenon has been of extreme interest to medical researchers. Unfortunately, it now appears that the species is extinct, only a bit over a decade after its discovery.

A pair of Eurasian common newts, *Triturus vulgaris*.
Photo by B. Kahl.

LIFE HISTORY OF THE ALPINE NEWT

One of the best known of the "typical" newts in continental Europe, the alpine newt, *Triturus alpestris*, has approximately seven subspecies ranging over much of central Europe, reaching the Atlantic coast in France and the Low Countries. It does not occur in Britain, but there is an isolated population in the Cantabrian Range in northwestern Spain. It is almost totally aquatic and is almost always found in or close to water. In the northern part of its range it occurs in a wide range of habitats, but it is most frequently found in woodland ponds and lakes. Southern populations are almost all montane, occurring in lakes and slower moving streams. The start of the breeding season varies with the part of the range, but in central Europe the newts congregate in the breeding ponds from early to mid-February. An increase in photoperiod combined with a rise in temperature triggers breeding activity. Unlike some related species, it seems to have little preference in the selection of breeding waters and may use shallow ditches just as successfully as deep, densely vegetated ponds and lakes.

Adult female alpine newts may reach a maximum of 12 cm (5 in) in length, with the males somewhat shorter. Both the male and the female have a uniformly bright orange or deep red undersurface. In the breeding season, a bluish or purplish hue may suffuse the normal dark gray to black color of the upper body in both sexes, but the male takes on a particularly sleek look, with his blue flanks, white cheeks spotted in black, and smooth crest.

An amorous male will attempt to attract a suitable female by performing a courtship dance, usually at a water depth of 20-30 cm (8-12 in) on the pond floor. The area of courtship is usually devoid of vegetation. The male will approach a prospective mate and nudge her. If she is not impressed by his advances, she will simply swim away, but if receptive she will stay her ground and await further developments. After "rubbing noses" with the female, the male will stiffen his body into a tight bow, pointing his tail tip in her direction. Next, he places his two forelimbs firmly onto the substrate or onto a weed to give him stability while he rapidly wriggles the rear part of his body and tail. At the same time his cloaca releases an "aphrodisiac" scent (pheromone) that is wafted in the direction of the female by water currents created by his own actions.

The performance often continues for many minutes. The female seems to become hypnotized by the male's actions, but more likely from the scent being wafted toward her. Eventually the male walks off on the substrate, closely followed by the female, still apparently transfixed. The male then deposits a spermatophore in front of the female and continues to walk, guiding the following female over the sperm packet, which is taken into her cloaca. As soon as this has occurred, the male seems to lose all further interest in the proceedings and usually swims off in search of a good meal. Inside the female the individual sperm break away from the

sperm mass and migrate into the upper parts of the cloaca, where they are stored in pockets of tissue in the cloacal walls. The female is able to preserve the sperm in this way for up to a year, and they are seated in the correct position to fertilize eggs as they descend from the ovaries.

The fertilized eggs are now ready to leave the vent, but first the female finds a suitable water plant. Taking a single leaf, she curls it with her rear limbs and, holding it with both feet, brings her vent into such a position that a single egg can be laid in the curl of the leaf. An adhesive substance that coats the egg causes it to adhere firmly below leaf, where it is relatively safely camouflaged and protected, but in an area rich in oxygen, which is very important to the development of the embryo.

In a few days the tiny larvae hatch. They are completely limbless and about 8 mm (0.35 in) in length. They possess three feathery external gills on either side of the neck just behind the head. At first the larvae do not feed as they are still absorbing the contents of

One of the most distinctive features of the alpine newt, *Triturus alpestris*, is the bright orange belly. Photo by L. Wischnath.

This interesting photo shows a *T. vulgaris* still encased in the egg. Photo by B. Kahl.

the yolk sac attached to the abdomen, but as soon as this is accomplished, they begin to hunt for tiny aquatic organisms, on which they will feed voraciously. The larvae gradually develop into recognizable little newts about 4 cm (1.6 in) long by the end of the summer. At this time some will leave the water to seek their fortunes on dry land, though others remain aquatic for most of the year. In some populations, notably in the eastern part of the range, alpine newts are neotenous and remain aquatic throughout the year.

For the remainder of the summer and the first part of the fall, terrestrial newts of all ages hunt out insects in the undergrowth, fattening themselves up for the period of hibernation that is to follow. During this time the newts are largely crepuscular (active at dawn and dusk) and nocturnal, hiding during the day under logs and ground debris, in root systems, and often in the burrows of other animals. The adults lose their breeding dress before leaving the water and revert to plain dark gray to black, but retain the reddish to orange undersurface. The

The two tiny creatures clinging to this leaf are newly hatched common newts, *T. vulgaris*. Photo by S. Damian.

bright colors of many salamander and newt species act as a warning to would-be predators that they are poisonous or distasteful. Most species possess skin glands that will release poisonous or irritant substances in times of danger. It is therefore advisable to wash your hands after handling salamanders as such substances can cause irritation and pain if transferred to the eyes and mucous membranes.

In most parts of its range the alpine newt spends the winter in hibernation. As the hours of daylight decrease and the temperatures diminish, both juvenile and adult newts seek out suitable spots in which to take their winter rest. Some may burrow deep down in loose earth, or use the burrows of other animals, until they reach a depth out of reach of the heaviest winter frosts. Others may hide in the mud at the bottom of their permanent ponds. Species that normally hibernate in the wild can be kept in captivity without hibernation simply by providing extra warmth and light in the winter. However, this confuses their natural rhythms, and then the animals are not only unlikely to breed, but the length of their life is likely to be correspondingly reduced. The cycle starts over again when the warmth and light of the springtime sun cause the newts to wake up and again congregate for another breeding season.

The well-known axolotl,
Ambystoma mexicanum.
Photo by L. Andres.

**LIFE CYCLE OF THE
AXOLOTL**

The life cycle of the axolotl,
Ambystoma mexicanum,
probably is better known than
that of any other species of
salamander. This is due to the
fact that, over the years, this
fascinating creature has
become almost domesticated.
It is not only the most common
of all "pet" amphibians, but
has been a popular medium
for biological research and
education. It is the only
salamander that may be legally
kept as a pet in Australia
(where it is commonly referred
to as the "Mexican walking
fish") and is, in fact, the only
salamander legally present in
that country outside zoos and
research establishments.

The Spanish conquistadors
who arrived in Mexico in the
16th century were probably
the first Europeans to see live
axolotls. The axolotl was said
to be partially sacred to the
original natives of the Lakes
Xochimilcho and Chalco areas
(near the present Mexico City),
but it still appeared on the
menu at certain times of the
year. Today, wild axolotls may
still be found in these same
lakes, but they now have
protected status. Because of
pollution and land
development, including lake
drainage and refilling, axolotls
are rare or absent in many
spots where they once were
common.

Although so well known, the
axolotl is an interesting
amphibian that deserves a
place in the collection of the
salamander keeper. It is
especially useful to the
beginner, being relatively easy
to keep, feed, and breed.
Another plus is that all
available specimens are

The axolotl is widely bred in captivity. This is a female with her eggs. Photo by P. W. Scott.

captive-bred, so there is no depletion of wild populations.

The axolotl has a broad, shovel-like snout and a flattened head with a wide mouth. Its small, lidless eyes are wide-spaced but oriented toward the top of the head. The short but robust limbs are spaced well apart on the sturdy body, which sports a number of vertical (costal) grooves along the flanks. There are four fingers and five toes respectively on the front and back limbs. A low crest starts just behind the head and runs along the vertebral column onto the laterally flattened tail, where it becomes wider. The crest also continues along the underside of the tail, and is used by the animal as an aid to swimming and steering. The limbs are not used for swimming but may assist in braking and steering. They are mostly used for walking about on the substrate. The axolotl's most prominent feature is the pair of three-lobed feathery gills that project up to 2 cm (0.8 in) on either side of the head. These are deep reddish brown in normal specimens but bright crimson in albinos.

A mature axolotl may be as long as 25 cm (10 in), though the average is more likely to be around 20 cm (8 in). The "normally" colored axolotl, like its wild counterpart, is dark sooty brown above, with darker brown to black blotches and flecks, and lighter beneath. Over the years a number of color mutations, including albinos, goldens, and pieds, have appeared in captive stocks. These have been cultured to the extent that they are all commonly available, The bicolored pied variety is probably the most attractive.

In the wild, axolotls are not known to metamorphose into terrestrial forms, but they can

Note the interesting gelatinous layer wrapped around these *A. mexicanum* eggs. Photo by M. Gilroy.

be persuaded to change into terrestrial adults in captivity. Normal specimens become dark gray with yellow spots, the tail becomes round in section, and the skin becomes smoother. This can be accomplished by gradually reducing the water

depth over a period of several months. Once the water is about 2 cm (0.8 in) deep, the animals will be forced to start taking atmospheric oxygen. The process can also be halted at any stage almost up to full metamorphosis by again increasing the water depth and allowing the partially absorbed gills to redevelop. However, once the gills have been completely absorbed the process is irreversible, and the salamander would drown if forcibly kept below water.

Metamorphosis evidently is influenced by the amount of thyroxine in the thyroid gland. If injected with a small quantity or immersed in a solution of this hormone, axolotls will develop into the terrestrial form. The introduction of minute quantities of iodine into the water in which axolotls are kept has been found to promote the production of thyroxine by the salamanders, also resulting in complete metamorphosis. The process of becoming adult while still looking like a larva and being able to reproduce in that state is known as neoteny, while such reproduction itself is known as pedogenesis.

Another outstanding property of the axolotl (shared with many other salamanders)

These axolotl eggs are only one day old. Photo by L. Andres.

is its ability to regenerate appendages that have been lost accidentally or to predators (the latter often being other, larger axolotls). A new appendage, usually perfect in every detail, will grow within a few weeks to replace the missing one.

Axolotls can be housed in simple aquaria, no more than four specimens to a tank of 60 x 30 cm (2 ft x 1 ft). Depth should be somewhere between 20 and 30 cm (8 to 12 in). Clean aquarium gravel and a few pebbles for decoration may be placed on the bottom. The tank should be equipped with an aerator and a filter. Supplementary heating is unnecessary as axolotls will fare well at room temperatures and can tolerate a range of temperatures, though they seem to thrive best at 17-20°C (63-68°F).

Wild axolotls will eat almost any living creature they can overpower. In captivity they will take lean raw meat, which they seem to find by a combination of smell and touch. This, however, does not constitute a balanced diet and should only be a supplement of various live foods, such as earthworms, slugs, snails, mealworms, crickets, etc. Do not over feed and allow uneaten food to remain in the tank as you will be asking for trouble (fouling, smells, pollution, and ultimately the death of your axolotls). In the absence of livefoods over a period, it is wise to work a good quality vitamin and

The tiger salamander, *Ambystoma tigrinum*, has proven fairly easy to breed in captivity. Photo by K. Lucas, Steinhart Aquarium.

mineral powder into the lean meat. See what your pet shop or veterinarian has to offer.

Wild axolotls breed in the springtime (usually February), when melting snows from surrounding mountains temporarily reduce temperatures in the lakes. In captivity this phenomenon can be simulated by adding ice cubes to the axolotl tank, thus subjecting the amphibians to thermal changes. This may be done at any time of the year, but most successes take place during the months of December to mid-July. Adult axolotls of both sexes are similar in size and shape, though the male may have a slightly broader head and the female a plumper body. When sexually mature, the male will also have a markedly swollen vent region. They may breed from the age of 18 months onward, but best results occur when the animals are 30 months old. As the animals age, they become less productive. Most captive axolotls will live six to ten years if given optimum conditions.

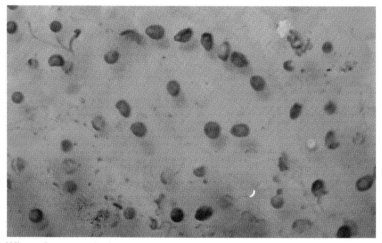

When these axolotls mature, they should be able to live in captivity for at least six years. Photo by P. W. Scott.

The male courts the female by making stylized movements with his body. These include bending the body almost double and rapidly wriggling the tail. Eventually he deposits a spermatophore on the substrate close to the female and then loses any further interest in the proceedings. The receptive female takes the spermatophore into her cloaca, where it will release sperm to fertilize the eggs as they are being laid. About 48 hours after mating, oviposition begins. Eggs are laid in batches of 10-30 on the leaves of water plants or on substrate debris until altogether 500-800 eggs are laid.

In captivity it is best to keep sexes separate until a breeding response is required. Then a single pair is housed together in a small tank. A temperature reduction from the normal 17-20°C down to 10-12°C (50-54°F) usually will result in almost immediate mating behavior. Egglaying can be expected within 48 hours. It is best to provide a number of pieces of plastic pipe (12 mm, 0.5 in, electrical conduit is ideal) jammed across the width of the container and at about half the water's depth, ensuring you leave plenty of room for the animals to swim between them. Most of the eggs will then be laid on these tubes. After laying, the adults can be

These are recently hatched *A. mexicanum* larvae. Photo by P. W. Scott.

returned to their respective stock tanks. The water temperature in the breeding tank can then be slowly raised back to 17-20°C. The water should be fresh, well-aerated, and free of chlorine. The eggs should hatch within 14 days. Any eggs that turn milky white are infertile and should be

These larvae are slightly more developed (two weeks) than the ones in the last photo. Photo by P. W. Scott.

capsules. They will not require food for the first 48 hours as they are still feeding from the yolk sac, but after this they may be given infusoria, brine shrimp, and water fleas. Pounded lean meat and hard-boiled egg yolk may also be given, but only in extremely small quantities to avoid pollution of the water. The larvae soon become active. At five days of age they should be separated into batches and placed in aerated containers of water about 20 cm (8 in) deep. Well-fed youngsters grow rapidly, and you will soon be able to give them larger food items such as tubifex, whiteworms, mosquito larvae, and small earthworms. Properly cared for and given a varied diet, young axolotls can reach sexual maturity in as little as six months, but for best results it is advisable to wait until they are nine to twelve months old before this is attempted.

removed with a pipette before they decay and pollute the water.

On hatching, the tiny axolotls remain close to the egg

CAECILIANS

In general it can be said that less is known about the breeding habits of caecilians than about the other amphibian groups. Most

This is a nest model of a yellow-striped caecilian, *Ichthyophis kohtaoensis.* Note the terrestrial burrowing site. Photo by R. G. Sprackland.

species are terrestrial and burrowing. Unique among the amphibians (with the possible exception of the frog *Ascaphus*), the male caecilian has a penis-like organ formed from the cloaca. Fertilization is therefore internal. In most species the female lays a relatively small number of eggs, though some species are ovoviviparous or viviparous. Oviparous species lay about 30 eggs in a moist subterranean chamber and the female curls around them. It seems that contact with the maternal body is in some way essential to the normal development of the eggs, as those removed from the mother never hatch.

GENERAL COMMENTS

Most amphibian species require external stimuli to bring them into breeding condition. Temperate species, for example, usually breed in the spring, shortly after hibernation, and are affected by increases in temperature, photoperiod, and light intensity. Tropical species may be influenced by changes in humidity, either seasonal or coincidental such as sudden downpours of rain in areas of protracted aridity. Some species can be persuaded to breed in captivity by injecting them with certain hormones. Like the clawed frogs (*Xenopus*), the Spanish or ribbed newt (*Pleurodeles waltl*) can be induced to spawn by injecting 250 International Units of H.C.G. (human chorionic gonadotrophin)

It is best to split newly metamorphosed animals into groups of ten or so and house them in small rearing terraria. This way you will be able to keep an eye on individuals and ensure that they are getting a fair share of food. It will also be easier to maintain satisfactory hygienic measures.

The little amphibians will require large numbers of tiny insects or spiders. Fruitflies are ideal for most species as they can be bred in large numbers, are small enough for

the tiny mouths to take, and are relatively nutritious. A good supply of young fruitflies will result in rapid growth until a greater variety of livefoods can be accepted. First instar crickets, houseflies, and insect sweepings are suitable for the second stage of feeding. Some small frog and salamander species never grow large enough to take food items much larger than fruitflies or first instar crickets, so foliage sweepings will be essential to ensure a balanced diet.

Above: **This attractive animal is known as Couch's spadefoot toad, *Scaphiopus couchii*. It is rarely bred in captivity. Photo by W. B. Allen, Jr.**

Left: **Many species, like this tiger salamander, *Ambystoma tigrinum*, require very exact climatic conditions in order to breed properly, but it can be done. Photo by R. T. Zappalorti.**

Classification of the Amphibia

The science of identifying and naming species is known as taxonomy, and the Swedish naturalist Karl von Linne (1707-1779) can be regarded as one of the fathers of the science. The binomial system originally consisted of applying a double Latin (or sometimes Latinized Greek or a mixture of the two languages) name to every species, one name indicating the genus, the other the species. The pioneer system was of course primitive by today's standards (Linnaeus included both the reptiles and amphibians in the class Amphibia!), but it set a precedent for the following generations of taxonomists who gradually improved it to its present form.

This does not, of course, mean that the system is infallible; taxonomists still argue today about the finer points of classification. There are many current disputes in force regarding the Amphibia.

The state of classification of the Amphibia is probably less well advanced than that of the higher tetrapods, especially among the frogs, and there are many years of work to be done before we can say that every problem is cleared up—if ever.

Natural classification is a hierarchical or layered ranking of animals or plants into different groups, based on differences and similarities between them. The bottom rank in this arrangement is the species (plural: species, always with the last s), one of a group of organisms that are all essentially the same, at least with very little variation, and which interbreed to produce more individuals of a similar type. A number of species that are not essentially similar but have several characteristics in common are grouped into a genus (plural: genera). Numbers of genera are placed into families, families into orders, orders into classes,

Photo of the treefrog *Trachycephalus jordani* by R. S. Simmons.

classes into phyla (plural of phylum) and so on. The numbers of similarities between members of a group become increasingly less at each step up the classification. For example, members of different genera within one family have less in common than species within a single genus. In extreme or difficult cases, additional categories such as subfamily or infraorder may be used.

Taxonomy, which includes the study of the theory, procedure, and rules of classification of organisms, is a complex subject that has caused much argument and controversy among scientists for generations. Modern classification is based on phylogeny (the history of evolution of a species, genus, etc.) as far as this is known, but in those groups where evolutionary information is sparse then it is supplemented with a degree of calculated guesswork.

Opposite: The "binomial" name of the Delaland's frog is *Tomopterna delalandii*. Photo by G. Dibley.

Below: Because classification changes often occur, it is not impossible that *Triturus cristatus* could be given an entirely different name in the future. Photo by M. Gilroy.

The binomial system devised by Linnaeus was eventually adopted universally and is still used today but in much improved form. Each new species discovered is given a two-part name, known as a binomial, made up of the generic name and the specific or trivial name, by the taxonomist who gives it its first scientific description (not necessarily the discoverer). Thus, in the species *Hyla arenicolor* (canyon tree frog), *Hyla* is the generic name, which is applied to all frogs in that genus (all 250 species of them) and *arenicolor* is the specific name, which is applied to a single species only. The name of the original author(s) and the year of description are written after the binomial; for example: *Hyla arenicolor* Cope, 1866; *Hyla crucifer* Wied-Neuwied, 1838; *Hyla regilla* Baird & Girard, 1852. In cases where the species has been renamed after revision, the author(s) of the original name are still retained, but in parentheses, for example: *Hyla arborea* (Linnaeus, 1758).

Sometimes species show geographical variation in color

or form. Such variations may not be sufficient to warrant separate specific classification, so they are classified as subspecies. In such cases a third name is added to the binomial, making it a trinomial. Subspecies will interbreed quite readily and indeed do so at the borders of their individual ranges, usually producing examples with characteristics from both groups; such individuals are known as intergrades. A good example of subspecific nomenclature is that applied to the North American tiger salamander, *Ambystoma tigrinum* of which six subspecies are usually recognized. These are the eastern, *A. t. tigrinum*; barred, *A. t. mavortium*; Arizona, *A. t. nebulosum*; blotched, *A. t. melanostictum*; gray, *A. t. diaboli*; and Sonora, *A. t. stebbinsi*. The original (nominate) subspecies has its specific name repeated in the trinomial (as in *A. t. tigrinum* above), while further subspecies receive a new subspecific name placed after the specific name. The rules of description and authors apply to subspecific names in the same way as to specific ones, thus: *Ambystoma tigrinum tigrinum* (Green, 1825).

Many herpetologists now question the validity of subspecies in many situations. They feel that subspecific status is provided to an animal as an alternative to investigating deeper into its natural history and relationships with related species: If you don't know much about the salamander but it looks different, just call it a subspecies. A real subspecies, assuming that such exist, would have well-defined characters that are not just extremes of characters represented in adjacent forms. It would have a restricted range of some type with only narrow intergradation. In fact, a "real" subspecies would be almost indistinguishable in the nature of its characters from a "true" species, making the value of the category doubtful.

In printed publications, generic, specific, and subspecific names are almost always written in italic script (or underlined when italic script is not available) to avoid confusion with common names

Because it is a subspecies, this barred tiger salamander has three Latin names: *Ambystoma tigrinum mavortium*. Photo by R. S. Simmons.

or with the text in which they are cited. This is particularly useful when a biologist or other interested person is studying papers or books written in a foreign language.

It will be noted that scientific names are often abbreviated. When a species is first mentioned in a text, the full scientific name (with or without its author) is usually given, but when the same name is repeated it is abbreviated. For example: *Discoglossus nigriventer* Mendelssohn & Steinitz, 1943, is abbreviated to *D. nigriventer*, while *Discoglossus pictus sardus* Tschudi, 1837, is abbreviated to *D. p. sardus*.

Frogs and Toads

The frogs and toads are members of the order Anura (tailless amphibians), sometimes referred to as the Salientia. Some diagnostic features of the Anura are as follows:

1. There is no tail in the adult (but see reference to *Ascaphus* later in the text).

2. There is no distinct neck and the head is apparently continuous with the body.

3. The hind limbs are fairly large and modified for jumping and/or swimming. The paired bones of the forearms and forelegs are fused.

4. The eyes are relatively large and the eyelids movable.

5. The ear-drum (tympanum) is usually prominent.

6. The skull is not completely roofed with bone.

7. The body is relatively short.

8. Most species are vocal, with a well-developed larynx; calls are characteristic of different species.

9. Both lungs are present and of similar size.

10. Fertilization is usually external and reproduction is usually oviparous (see species descriptions for some exceptions)

As there are over 3500 species in the order, it is not possible to list them all in a volume of this size. Some descriptions will be more detailed than others, often depending on the popularity of a particular species or, in some cases, availability of accessible information.

FAMILY BUFONIDAE

The typical toad with its dry, warty skin is a member of the genus *Bufo* in the family Bufonidae, but there are also many genera with species not externally resembling the typical toads. This is one of the largest of the anuran families, containing some 25 genera and over 330 species found in most parts of the world with the exception of Australasia, Madagascar, and most oceanic islands, although

This highly attractive male toad hails from Costa Rica and is known as *Bufo luetkeni*. Photo by P. Freed.

artificial introductions (see *Bufo marinus*) have seen toads successfully colonize even some of these habitats. The genus *Bufo* alone contains over 200 species, most of which are typically "toad-like"; many are extremely difficult to distinguish from each other. Many species in this family make excellent terrarium animals that soon settle down in captivity.

Atelopus is a large genus containing at least 44 species, none of which externally look as though they could possibly be related to toads! Most are smooth-skinned. Many are attractively colored and make good terrarium subjects. They are mostly slender with relatively long and thin limbs. The skin secretions are poisonous, varying in potency from species to species. They are found in Central and South America from Costa Rica to Bolivia, with isolated species in eastern Brazil and the Guianas. Most are terrestrial and diurnal. Most species breed in temporary ponds and puddles after heavy rains; eggs hatch in 24 hours and complete metamorphosis takes place in a relatively short time. Habitats vary immensely from species to species, and terrarium care will reflect on the area of natural habitat,

especially with regard to temperatures. Species from high mountainous areas, for example, will require little if any artificial heating. *A. boulengeri*, from medium altitudes in Ecuador and Colombia, grows to 3.5 cm (1.5 in) and is variably reddish with brown markings. *A. varius*, from Costa Rica and Panama to Colombia, also grows to 3.5 cm (1.5 in) and is highly variable in color but usually shows a mixture of bright yellow, orange, and brown. The particularly colorful (cadmium-yellow with black enamel-like blotches) and attractive subspecies *A. v. zeteki* is classified in Appendix I in CITES (Convention on International Trade in Endangered Species of Flora and Fauna), which means it is considered to be endangered

Facing page: Top: Certain species of frogs, such as this Atelopus varius, vary greatly in color. Photo by P. Freed. Bottom: Black toads, Bufo exsul, are hardy and make good pets but are almost never available. Photo by K. Lucas, Steinhart Aquarium.

and therefore strictly protected in its wild habitat.

Bufo is the largest genus in the family and has a fairly cosmopolitan distribution but is absent from Madagascar, Australasia, and Oceania (except for artificially introduced populations of *B. marinus*). Species of *Bufo* are found in a wide range of habitats, from tropical rain forest to semi-desert. Most species have the typical, warty toad-like appearance which you either love or hate! Many species are plain earthy-brown in color, but some have quite attractive patterns and colors. Their most endearing quality is probably their character, most species being seemingly "intelligent" and even "affectionate."

Bufo bufo is the "original toad" of Europe, first scientifically described by Linnaeus as *Rana bufo*. Found

This attractive little fellow is known as the common European toad, *Bufo bufo*. Photo by G. Dibley.

The western toad, *Bufo boreas*, lives up to its English name and is found in many parts of western North America. Photo by R. Haas.

in suitable habitats in most of Europe and extending far into Asia, this species is a typical example of what the average person expects a toad to look like. Growing to about 10 cm (4 in) in the northern—and 15 cm (6 in) in the southern—part of its range, the toad has a plump, robust body, relatively short arms and legs, and webbed feet. The large golden eyes have horizontal pupils. The skin is dry to the touch and covered with numerous "warts," including the typically large parotoid glands on either side of the neck that produce an irritable poisonous exudate that is very effective in protecting toads from predators. Once a carnivore has had a mouthful of angry toad, he is never likely to try the experiment again! In color, the upper side of the toad is a mottled mixture of browns or grays and may take on a reddish or yellowish tinge, to resemble the color of the earth in which it lives. The throat and underside are off-white, mottled with dark gray to brown.

Like most toads, this species spends the greater part of the year on dry land, holing up under a rock or log during the day and setting forth to forage

This interesting photo is showing the egg strands of *Bufo bufo*. Photo by L. Wischnath.

bursts of relative speed with rapid hops, usually when alarmed. Most toads make very satisfying and endearing "pets," quickly settling into terrarium life; they are also relatively intelligent, at least in anuran circles. This species can be kept in an unheated terrarium with a few potted plants and hiding places such as stone caves, hollow logs, or broken crocks. The substrate can consist of a mixture of peat, sand, and leaf litter, kept very slightly damp. Outside the breeding season, a small water dish is adequate to allow the toads to treat themselves to an occasional soak.

Maintain the temperature preferably below 22°C (72°F); in temperate areas, this may be allowed to reduce itself to natural levels at night. Food consists of a variety of invertebrates. As toads are somewhat gluttonous, the meals should be regulated to prevent the onset of obesity. A winter hibernation period of two to three months at 4-5°C (39-41°F) will help bring the toads into spring breeding condition. In the wild, this species breeds in early spring.

for invertebrates at night. It normally walks a few paces, then stops as if contemplating its next move before moving on. However, it also is capable of

A healthy African red toad, *Bufo carens*, of adult breeding size. Photo by K. Lucas, Steinhart Aquarium.

The males assemble first at suitable ponds, the females arriving a few days later. Males often outnumber the females by as much as 5 to 1. This is believed to be a natural breeding strategy that ensures that each female receives attention from a healthy, fertile male. The male grasps the female in amplexus, holding firmly around the thoracic region just behind her arms, and the pair move about as the female lays a double "string" of eggs that may be wound around water plants or other submerged objects such as bicycle frames or bedsteads. After spawning, the females leave the water immediately to spend another year on the land; the males may stay in the water for a few more days, perhaps in the hope of getting another female.

The eggs hatch in a few days and the larvae develop into tiny toads by late summer. The newly metamorphosed toadlets leave the water in great numbers as soon as suitable weather arrives. Humid or rainy weather will often result in the "plague" of toads that you often hear about. *B. bufo* is unlikely to breed in the confines of an indoor terrarium and is more likely to do so in the relatively large pond of a cool greenhouse or an outdoor enclosure.

Bufo americanus is one of at least 18 species of North American bufonid toads. Known as the American toad, *B. americanus* is the one most familiar to inhabitants of the eastern USA. Superficially similar to *B. bufo* in appearance, this species grows to 11 cm (4.5 in) in length. There are three rather poorly defined subspecies. The colors range from brown to brick red above, patterned with lighter colors. There is sometimes a light vertebral stripe. It is found in the eastern part of North America from central Canada through to the southern states (but not reaching the Gulf Coast, where it is replaced by the southern toad, *B. terrestris*). Its habits and breeding requirements are very similar to those of the European toad, and it requires similar housing and care. Other North American toads requiring similar care (but always taking the climatic factors of the natural habitat into consideration) include the Great Plains toad, *B. cognatus*; American green toad, *B. debilis*; Canadian toad, *B. hemiophrys*; and the particularly common and wide-ranging Woodhouse's toad, *B. woodhousei*. The attractive subspecies *B. woodhousei fowleri*, with its light and dark pattern, is common over much of the eastern United States and is particularly popular as a terrarium inmate.

Bufo blombergi, Blomberg's toad, is a large species native to northern Ecuador and southwestern Colombia. It was first described in 1951. Growing to 23 cm (9.25 in), it soon became popular as a terrarium exhibit and has been regularly bred in zoological collections. In addition to its size, its colors enhance its attraction; it is cream to golden-brown above and steel gray to black along the flanks and below, including the limbs. In captivity it requires a large terrarium with a deep pool for breeding. Maintain the temperature in the range of 22-28°C (72-82°F) and feed on a

This is an example of the red phase of *Bufo americanus*, which is normally some shade of brown. Photo by R. T. Zappalorti.

variety of large invertebrates, pink mice, small fishes, etc.

Bufo boreas, the North American western toad, replaces *B. americanus* in the West. It inhabits the Pacific Coast from southern Alaska to Baja California and east to Alberta, Montana, Wyoming, Utah, Colorado, and Nevada, inhabiting an obviously wide range of habitats. There are three well-defined subspecies and a great color variety from greenish or brownish to grayish with reddish warts, often surrounded with black blotches and with a light-colored dorsal stripe. Usually nocturnal, but may be active during the day

One-month-old offspring of the giant toad, *Bufo marinus*. Photo by M. Gilroy.

when nighttime temperatures are excessively low. Captive housing and care are similar to *B. bufo* but, of course, the temperature and humidity requirements of the toad's natural habitats must be taken into consideration.

Bufo calamita, the natterjack or running toad, is a small species growing to 7.5 cm (3 in). Native to western and central Europe and extending into western Russia, it is a robust, short-limbed toad that runs in short bursts rather than walking or jumping. It is usually brownish in color, but has an attractive yellow dorsal stripe, and some of its warts may sometimes be reddish orange. In the wild it is typically found in sandy areas, where it breeds in shallow, heathland pools. It may even be found near the seashore and has been known to breed in brackish water. Keep it in a large terrarium with sandy substrate and a large water bath. Supplementary heating is unnecessary under normal circumstances. In Britain, the natterjack has become rare, probably due to loss of habitat, and it now is under protection there as an endangered species.

Bufo marinus, the giant, marine, or cane toad, warrants a special mention. Typically toad-like with a dry, warty skin, it has extremely large parotoid glands. Its poison is especially potent, and the animal grows to a length of 25 cm (10 in) in length! Although most people regard it as ugly and noxious, frog-lovers treat it as a prize pet. Indeed, this species can become as near to being a pet as any amphibian could. It becomes tame, trusting, and even gets to recognize its owner. It is one of the few species that will take inanimate food, and some fanciers delight in fattening up their specimens with dog or cat food or even raw steak! The author was recently introduced to a large female of

Although many species of *Bufo* often are seen in collections, certain others, like this unique-looking *Bufo typhonius* are not. Photo by J. Visser.

this species weighing 1.6 kilograms (about 3.6 lb.)!

This toad usually is a uniform gray-brown to reddish brown with a lighter underside. Juvenile specimens may be substantially and often quite prettily marked with lighter colors, but these are lost as the toad grows. The enormous parotoid glands extend down the sides of the neck and thorax from just behind the eyes. As in most other toads, they release a milky fluid when the toad is roughly handled. This fluid is highly toxic, will burn the eyes and mucous membranes, and, in some people, will irritate the skin. The hands should always be carefully washed after handling any amphibian, but especially after dealing with this one. A dog or cat that tries to savage a giant toad can even die from the effects of the poison, so don't mix your toads with your other pets!

The natural range of the giant toad is Central America and northern South America. It extends slightly into the USA in southern Texas and has become feral in southern Florida after being introduced. The predatory habits of this species have, in the past, led to its being introduced to many other parts of the world as a potential controller of agricultural pests. In some areas it has not only failed to carry out the job it was introduced for, but it has also colonized so successfully that it has become a pest in its own right, threatening native fauna by displacement and poisoning of domestic animals. In Australia, where it was introduced from Hawaii (where it had been introduced in 1932) in 1935 to combat the pests of sugar cane, it is now considered to be a serious threat to many native amphibians and reptiles that it may devour and/or displace. At the time of writing, a campaign to eradicate the toad is in operation in the city of Brisbane (capital of Queensland, Australia). This consists of numbers of people wearing gloves and armed with

This female giant toad, *Bufo marinus*, is from Florida and would make a good captive. Photo by R. T. Zappalorti.

plastic bags going out at night and collecting as many toads as possible. These are then killed by deep freezing. The giant toad is a prohibited animal in several areas.

Like other toads, the giant toad is primarily nocturnal. Sale of this animal is prohibited in a number of places. Photo by R. T. Zappalorti.

This toad is primarily nocturnal, coming out at night to hunt. During dry periods it will estivate, while in colder areas it may hibernate for three or four months, usually burrowing about 15-30 cm (6-12 in) below the surface. The toads are commonly attracted to street or porch lights at night, where they will congregate in groups, waiting to snap up any unfortunate insects when they fall to the ground. Those individuals that prefer their food barbecued have taken to sitting below the electronic "insectocuters" or "bug zappers" that have become so popular in suburbia in tropical and subtropical areas!

The marine toad is a very easy captive and can be kept in a large terrarium or even given the run of the house. It likes a water bath, in which it will soak in hot weather. Temperatures up to 28°C (82°F) during the day and reduced to about 20°C (68°F) at night are suitable. Feed on a variety of larger invertebrates (grasshoppers, earthworms, beetles, moths) and small vertebrates (pink mice, small fish, etc.). It can be trained to take such things as lean meat and dog food from the fingers. This species is unlikely to breed in a small terrarium, but will do so in a large heated (22-28°C, 72-82°F) pool. Like *Xenopus*, it can be induced to breed with hormone injections and has in the past been used for pregnancy tests in some parts of the world. In countries where the toad is ubiquitous, it has replaced other frog species as educational material for anatomical studies.

Bufo melanostictus, the black-spotted toad, is the common toad of tropical southeastern Asia, ranging from the Himalayas to Sri Lanka and China to Indonesia. Growing to 10 cm (4 in), it is reddish brown with yellowish markings and with black tips to the warts. It occurs in many habitats, from sea level to over 3000 m (10,000 ft) and from urban to remote areas. It is a relatively easy and endearing terrarium subject. As it is usually specimens from the more tropical locations that find themselves in terraria, this should be reflected in the climatic conditions provided.

Bufo quercicus, the oak toad, is the smallest North American toad. It occurs in the USA from southeastern Virginia through all of Florida and to southeastern Louisiana, inhabiting pine and oak scrub country. Maximum size is 3.5 cm (1.25 in). It is a diminutive but attractive diurnal species colored in a mixture of browns

These two attractive toads, *Bufo regularis* (top), and *Melanophryniscus stelzneri*, both might make interesting pets, but they are not often seen on the commercial market. Photos by J. Coborn (top) and R. S. Simmons (bottom).

with a white or yellow vertebral stripe. It requires a terrarium with a sandy substrate and temperatures to 28°C (82°F), which can be reduced somewhat in the winter.

Bufo regularis is the African leopard toad, found in Africa south of the Sahara, where it is the best known toad.

Usually it is a species of grassland and open forest. Growing to 11 cm (4.5 in), it is light to dark brown with black, often square or rectangular, spots. It will settle well into a medium-sized, tropical, semi-humid terrarium.

Bufo viridis, the Eurasian green toad, is very colorful and thus is popular with terrarium keepers. Its cream to brown background color is marked with vivid olive-green to grass-green patches. Its care is similar to that of the common toad,

though summer warmth to around 26°C (79°F) is recommended.

Melanophryniscus contains about eight species in South America. All are terrestrial, flattened, and short-limbed. *M. moreirae* from southeastern Brazil reaches 2.5 cm (1 in) and is quite attractive, with bright yellow flecks on a dark background, while the underside is plain yellow. It requires a semi-humid tropical terrarium. It is a rainy season breeder.

Pedostibes is a genus of about six species of bufonids native to Southeast Asia. A popular terrarium subject is *P. hosii* from Malaysia and Indonesia. Growing to 10 cm (4 in) (female, male somewhat shorter), it has a granular skin, large orange eyes with horizontal pupils, and large adhesive finger and toe pads. It is mainly smoky brown to black with bright yellow flecks. This species requires a humid rainforest aquaterrarium with temperatures of 25-30°C (77-86°F).

FAMILY CENTROLENIDAE

A family with two genera confined to Central and South America from southern Mexico to northeastern Argentina, Brazil, and Bolivia. Most species are treefrog-like in appearance, with spade-shaped suction disks on the fingers and toes.

Centrolene is a monotypic genus separated from *Centrolenella* due mostly to the size of the single species. *Centrolene geckoideum* reaches 8 cm (3.25 in), more than twice as long as any *Centrolenella* species and much heavier in build. *C. geckoideum* is native to the Pacific Andean slopes of Colombia and Ecuador. It is more or less plain brown in color and treefrog-like in appearance. Little is known of its habits. It probably requires high humidity and temperatures not greater than 22°C (72°F), cooler at night.

Centrolenella is the main genus of the family, containing over 60 species. They are sometimes referred to as glass frogs or ghost frogs due to the translucent appearance of the skin; the intestines and heart often are clearly visible through the belly skin. Most species are arboreal and nocturnal. Spawn is deposited in foliage overhanging water, into which the larvae fall when they hatch. *C. euknemos* is found from Costa Rica and Panama to northern Colombia. Growing to only 2.5 cm (1 in), it is grass green with small black spots above, yellow beneath. It requires a tropical rainforest terrarium with temperature in the range of 22-28°C (72-82°F). It feeds on a variety of very small invertebrates.

FAMILY DENDROBATIDAE

A family with four genera native to Central and South America and including the poison dart, dart poison, or arrow poison frogs that secrete a sometimes particularly virulent poison from the pores of the skin. The prepared poison from four or five species is used by some Amerindian tribes to tip the points of their blowgun darts. (Thus the change from the old name of arrow poison frogs to dart poison frogs; these Amerindians use blowgun darts for hunting, not arrows.) The poison helps the hunters

Note the almost transparent nature of this *Centrolenella*'s skin. Perhaps this is why it is commonly known as a "ghost frog". Photo by R. S. Simmons.

subdue and kill prey such as monkeys. Reproduction of dendrobatids takes place on land. After sometimes fairly complicated courtship procedures, usually a small number of eggs are laid on a leaf or stone, or a cleared area of soil. After fertilizing the eggs the male guards them and keeps them moist until they hatch. He then maneuvers the larvae onto his back and transports them to water (usually a small cup of water as found in a bromeliad funnel or a tree hollow; *Colostethus* normally uses running water), where they continue to develop in the usual manner.

Colostethus is a genus containing more than 60 species native to the jungles of Central and South America. Unlike *Dendrobates* and *Phyllobates*, they do not secrete poison and are less colorful. Most species are less than 3 cm (1.25 in) in length. *C. inguinalis* is found from Colombia to Panama. Length 3 cm (1.25 in). It is brown to olive above and black on the flanks, the two colors being separated by a whitish stripe. *C. nubicola* is found from Costa Rica to Colombia and is very tiny at 2.2 cm (0.75 in). It is brown with light dorsolateral stripes and black flanks. Habits and care of *Colostethus* species are generally similar to *Dendrobates*.

Dendrobates is the oldest genus of poison dart frogs and now includes most of the species formerly assigned to *Phyllobates*. All 50 or so species are small (maximum length 5 cm, 2 in), and most are brightly colored. The skin glands secrete highly toxic substances. Like many other poisonous creatures, dendrobatid frogs like to draw attention to themselves and are diurnal and brightly colored. The bizarre coloration and interesting habits have put them in great demand as terrarium subjects, so much so that there has been an over-collection of some species from the wild. Fortunately, protective legislation has now helped alleviate the issue and improvements in captive care and breeding have kept a small but steady supply available of several species.

Dendrobates species may be kept in a small terrarium with high humidity and temperatures between 20 and 30°C (68-86°F), depending on the wild habitat. There is no need for a body of water other than water-holding bromeliads, though an aquarium heater in a jar of water will provide

This is the absolutely breathtaking "pallid" form of the Dyeing Poison Arrow Frog, *Dendrobates tinctorius*, from Surinam. Photo by R. D. Bartlett.

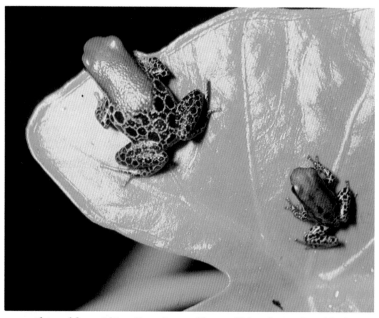

warmth and humidity. Regular mist spraying should be carried out. *Dendrobates* feed on a variety of small invertebrates, including fruitflies, ants, and termites. A few of the more popular and readily available species include: *D. auratus*, from Nicaragua and Panama to Colombia, patterned in metallic green to blue and black; *D. histrionicus*, from western Colombia and northwestern Ecuador, which is highly

Above: This photo should give you some idea of just how tiny most *Dendrobates* (this is *D. reticulatus*) are. Photo by H. Zimmermann.

Opposite: Sometimes the females of the genus *Phyllobates* will demonstrate what are known as "mating interference" actions. Photo of *P. terribilis* by H. Zimmermann.

variable in color but usually patterned in brown, yellow, and red; *D. lehmanni*, from Colombia, with wide enamel-like alternating red and black bands across the body; and *D. pumilio*, found from Nicaragua to Panama, red with tiny black or dark blue spots, and hind limbs blue with black markings. *D. tinctorius*, from northern Brazil and the Guianas, at 5 cm (2 in) is the largest species in the genus; it has wide black and yellow bands across body and blue hind limbs with black blotches.

Phyllobates, as presently restricted, is a genus of about five species that are similar in many respects to *Dendrobates* and require similar care in captivity. *P. bicolor* from the western Andes of Colombia is orange above, dark brown beneath, while *P. lugubris* from Panama and Costa Rica is black with two broad golden stripes along either side of the back, the flanks and limbs marbled with jade green. The most dangerous species of the genus, *Phyllobates terribilis*, is almost uniformly orangish. These frogs are not dangerous to humans under normal circumstances.

The Midwife Toad, *Alytes obstetricians*, in what is known as "lumbar amplexus." Photo by R. Guyetant, courtesy Dr. D. Terver, Nancy Aquarium, France.

FAMILY DISCOGLOSSIDAE

Containing five genera and about 13 species, the family is characterized by having a tongue that cannot be extended as in most other anuran families. Food is simply grabbed in the mouth and usually pushed into the gullet with the forelimbs.

Alytes is a genus containing only two species. *A. obstetricans*, with a length of 5 cm (2 in), is commonly known as the midwife toad due to its breeding habits. Mating and oviposition occur entirely out of water. The male attracts a female with his call and then clasps her just behind her forelimbs. She lays 20-40 eggs in a string that are fertilized by the male and then wound around his rear limbs. The eggs are carried about by the male for protection and are occasionally moistened by taking them into shallow pools or puddles. When ready to hatch, the eggs are deposited in a small body of water and the tadpoles develop in the normal manner, though they grow to a large size before metamorphosis and the toadlets are relatively big.

The midwife toad is a plump anuran with large eyes and vertical pupils. The color usually is gray, olive, or brown with darker markings. It occurs in western Europe from central Germany south into the Iberian peninsula, frequenting woodlands, parks, gardens, and quarries. Mainly nocturnal, the male calls with a bell-like tone (it is sometimes called "bell toad"). In captivity it requires a fairly large terrarium with a small water container and plenty of cover for it to hide during the day. Maintain at 22-25°C (72-77°F), reduced to 15°C (59°F) at night. Allow it to hibernate in winter. The other species of the genus is the Iberian midwife toad, *A. cisternasii*, which has similar habits and requires similar care, though it can probably which are native to Europe and Asia. One of the best known species, growing to a length of 5 cm (2 in), is *B. bombina*, commonly known as the fire-bellied toad due to the coloration on the underside.

Some members of the genus *Bombina* have become very common pets in recent years. Shown here is *Bombina orientalis*. Photo by Dr. H. Grier.

tolerate higher (to 28°C, 82°F) summer daytime temperatures. Both species would require spacious outdoor housing if breeding is contemplated.

Bombina is a genus of small, mainly aquatic, toad-like anurans, the six species of These little toads are extremely attractive and make good terrarium exhibits. The warty body is grayish green to black above, while the belly is black marked with vivid scarlet. It occurs in eastern Europe from Denmark to Bulgaria and

This little fellow is the Painted Frog, or *Discoglossus pictus*, and is related to Fire-bellied and Midwife Toads. Photo by R. Guyetant, courtesy Dr. D. Terver, Nancy Aquarium, France.

eastwards into Asia. Almost totally aquatic, it inhabits a variety of waters including ponds, marshes, rivers, streams, and ditches. It is mainly diurnal but may also be active at night. It spends much of its time floating on the water surface with limbs spread, catching floating insects. It requires a large aquaterrarium with rather more water than land. The water should be not less than 15 cm (6 in) deep and should be filtered and aerated. Aquatic plants may be used for decoration and refuge for the toads. Maintain the temperature in the range of 22-25°C (72-77°F), reduced a little at night. A winter hibernation period is beneficial. With optimum conditions it will breed in the terrarium. Eggs are laid in clumps of about 100 and should be removed into a separate container of (preferably) pond water that is aerated. The tadpoles will feed on suspended matter in the pond water. The closely related yellow-bellied toad, *B. variegata*, from western Europe, and the Oriental fire-bellied toad, *B. orientalis*, from the Far East, require similar husbandry.

Discoglossus pictus reaches a length of 7 cm (2.75 in). Although in the family of midwife and fire-bellied toads, this species, commonly known as the painted frog, is much more frog-like in appearance. It has a smooth, slippery skin and relatively long hind legs. The color is extremely variable, ranging through gray, brown, yellowish, or reddish above, with darker, often light-edged

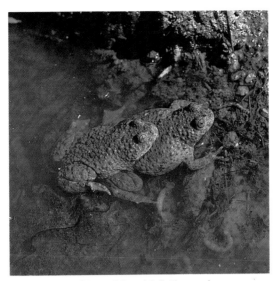

"Lumbar amplexus," in which the male grasps the female at the base of the hind legs, is considered a primitive behavior. These *Bombina variegata* were photographed by R. Guyetant, courtesy Dr. D. Terver, Nancy Aquarium, France.

spots and blotches. There is sometimes a pale vertebral stripe. The underside is whitish with darker speckling. It is native to southwestern Europe and North Africa, where it may be active by day or night and is usually found in the vicinity of permanent water including streams, ditches, ponds, and cisterns. It requires a large aquaterrarium with more water than land. Maintain at around 25°C (77°F), reduced for hibernation in the winter. It is most likely to breed in outdoor enclosures or greenhouses with deep water. The closely related *D. sardus*, the Tyrrhenian painted frog of Sardinia, Corsica, and some other Mediterranean islands, requires similar care.

Treefrogs, such as this *Hyla cipoensis* from Brazil, are interestingly patterned and often make hardy, undemanding captives. Photo by I. Sazima.

FAMILY HELEOPHRYNIDAE

A small family containing just one genus and four species all native to South Africa. Formerly treated as a subfamily of the Leptodactylidae, it was given familial status in 1976.

FAMILY HEMISIDAE

Containing a single genus and about eight species, the family is endemic to sub-Saharan Africa. Formerly given subfamilial status in the Hyperoliidae or sometimes placed in the Ranidae, it was raised to familial status in 1979.

FAMILY HYLIDAE

This is one of the larger anuran families, containing four subfamilies and some 37 genera. It includes many of those species commonly known as treefrogs, but by no means are all of the 640 or so species arboreal, some being surface-dwellers or even burrowers. Many of the treefrogs make ideal terrarium inmates. There is room here only to suggest a few species.

Subfamily Hemiphractinae

This subfamily contains seven genera of frogs with bizarre breeding habits.

Gastrotheca, the marsupial frogs, are the best known members of the subfamily. There are over 40 species, including *G. marsupiata*, which is found in the Amazonian drainage systems of the Andes from central Peru to southern Bolivia. Growing to 6 cm (2.5 in), it is fairly robust, with a wide snout and relatively long, partially webbed toes. It is a good climber but also spends a good deal of time on the ground. Variable from light green to brown in color with darker markings above; the underside is whitish with or

An uncommonly seen pet, this *Gastrotheca marsupiata*, one of the marsupial frogs, hails from the Amazon regions of Peru and southern Bolivia. Photo by H. Zimmermann.

without brown flecks. The male fertilizes the eggs as they are laid, and the female shovels them with her hind legs into the pouch on her back. The pouch opening faces to the rear and is situated above and close to the cloaca. The female carries the eggs for

40-50 days before depositing the hatched larvae in water. With some species in the genus, for example *G. ovifera*, complete metamorphosis from egg to fully formed froglet occurs in the maternal pouch. Care is as described for *Fritziana*.

Hemiphractus is a genus of five species that are not often seen in the terrarium but are bizarre and potentially excellent terrarium specimens. A good example is *H. bubalus*, a terrestrial frog from the upper Amazon basin. It has a large triangular head with a pointed snout and a helmet-like extension at the rear. The upper eye-lids end in a point. The color is a marbling of light and dark brown. Breeding habits are similar to those of some *Gastrotheca* species except that the eggs sink into individual hollows on the female's back, where they develop to complete metamorphosis much as in some *Pipa* species. These strange frogs require a large terrarium with high humidity and temperatures in the range of 22-28°C (72-82°F). Feed on a variety of small invertebrates.

May be aggressive toward other frogs or even other members of its own species.

Subfamily Hylinae

This subfamily contains some 23 genera, many doubtfully distinct or poorly defined. Recently there has been a move to break the large genus *Hyla*, the "typical" treefrogs, into several smaller groups. At the same time, several small genera have been merged with larger genera by some workers. For these reasons the generic limits in this subfamily are currently uncertain and likely to change rapidly in the near future.

Acris contains just two species. *A. gryllus*, with a length of 3 cm (1.25 in), is commonly known as the southern cricket frog. It occurs in the coastal plain of the eastern United States from southeastern Virginia to eastern Louisiana and inhabits marshes, lakes, streams, and ditches. The skin is warty and highly variable in color from brown, red, or green to almost black. There is a dark triangle between the eyes and long, dark stripes on the thighs. A

This creature is the southern cricket Frog, *Acris gryllus dorsalis*. It comes in many colors besides the green shown here. Photo by R. D. Bartlett.

diurnal, active species, it requires a medium-sized aquaterrarium with summer temperatures to 28°C (82°F), with a reduction at night and a winter rest period. Its close relative, *A. crepitans*, the northern cricket frog, requires similar conditions; its range (regardless of the common name) is much wider than its cousin, extending from the Great Lakes south through the central United States to the Mexican border and northeastward to southern New York.

Anotheca spinosa is a bizarre member of a monotypic genus. Growing to 7.5 cm (3 in), it has unusual spiny appendages on the head formed by extensions of the skull bones. These develop only as the animal reaches maturity. The large, high-set eyes have bronze-colored irises. The main color is brown with light-edged darker patches. Eggs are laid in small bodies of water, often in the water reservoirs of bromeliads.

by far the largest genus in the family, with over 250 species found in Eurasia, North Africa, and the Americas. Most are typical treefrogs with well-

Without a doubt, some of the most popular pet frogs are members of the genus *Hyla*, the common treefrogs. Shown here is the European treefrog, *Hyla arborea*. Photo by G. Dibley.

It ranges from southeastern Mexico to Costa Rica and Panama. It requires a well ventilated terrarium with facilities to climb and to hide. Maintain at about 25°C (77°F), with a reduction at night. A variety of invertebrate food is important to maintain good health and promote breeding.

Hyla (in the broad sense) is

developed adhesive discs on the tips of the fingers and toes. Many species from this genus are frequently kept as terrarium animals.

Hyla arborea, a plump little frog with smooth skin, grows to about 5 cm (2 in) and is commonly known as the European treefrog. It usually is bright green on the back with a

Of all the treefrogs, perhaps the green treefrog, *Hyla cinerea,* is the most popular. Photo by R. T. Zappalorti.

dark stripe running from each eye down the side of the body, though it can change quite dramatically to brown or yellowish depending on its situation and mood. It occurs in most of Europe except for the north and extends into Asia as far as the Caspian Sea. It requires husbandry similar to that for the American *H. cinerea*, as do two similar and closely related species, the stripeless treefrog, *H. meridionalis* from southern Europe and N. Africa, and the

Japanese treefrog, *H. japonica* from eastern Asia.

Hyla cinerea, which grows to a length of 5 cm (2 in), is known in the USA as the green treefrog. It is found in the southern and southeastern USA. Predominantly green above, it has a dark-edged, broad white stripe extending along the upper lip and about half-way along the body. Mainly nocturnal, it lives in foliage near permanent water, often resting on the undersides of large leaves. It requires a tall terrarium with large-leaved plants and a climbing log. The container should be kept fairly humid, with good ventilation. The daytime temperature can reach 27°C (81°F), but should be reduced at night to about 20°C (68°F). Feed on various species of flies, crickets, moths, and other small to medium-sized invertebrates. A period of reduced temperature at about 10°C (50°F) for a couple of months will simulate hibernation and increase chances of breeding. This, however, is more likely to be successful in a greenhouse with a suitable pond rather than in the confines of a relatively small terrarium. Other examples of North American species with similar requirements are the gray treefrogs, *H. versicolor* and *H. chrysoscelis*, and the squirrel treefrog, *H. squirella.*

Hyla crepitans is a treefrog occurring from Panama and Honduras into northern South America. Growing to 7 cm (2.75 in), it has a very slender body and a relatively large, flat head. The eye is conspicuous with its horizontal pupil and sea-green iris. The toes are fully webbed, and the adhesive pads of the fingers and toes are well developed. The color of the back is reddish to whitish, marbled with brown, giving it the appearance of a decaying leaf. A nocturnal species living in thick vegetation, it requires a tall, planted, humid terrarium with temperatures of 23-27°C (73-81°F). Feed it a variety of small invertebrates.

Hyla crucifer, the spring peeper, is one of the best known North American hylids, occurring through the eastern half of the continent from central Canada down to the Gulf Coast. In its range, the high pitched pipping call of the male frog is recognized as one of the first signs of spring. Its maximum length is just 3.5 cm (1.5 in), though it is usually smaller. It may be reddish, grayish, or dark brown in color, and is characterized by a darker brown X-shaped mark on the back. Like most treefrogs, this little fellow has large, flat, sucker-like toe pads to enable it to get a grip on the foliage of low trees and shrubs, often near or overhanging water. It requires a small but

Notice the greatly enlarged fingerpads on this blacksmith treefrog, *Hyla faber*. Photo by R. S. Simmons.

tall terrarium with a potted shrub and a pool of water. Supplementary heating is unnecessary unless southern specimens are kept in northern areas. Feed it on small invertebrates, including baby crickets and fruitflies. Recently this species has been moved from *Hyla* to *Pseudacris*, the chorus frogs, on the basis of skeletal characters and other factors.

Hyla faber is a South American species native to Brazil and Argentina, where it is a popular and well-known species. It is commonly known as the blacksmith frog, due to its metallic sounding call being likened to that of a hammer striking an anvil. It grows to 9 cm (3.5 in) and has a large, flattened head with a very wide mouth. It is brownish with a dark, irregular vertebral stripe; the underside is ocher-brown. It requires a warm (23-28°C, 78-82°F) planted terrarium with high humidity. Like just a few other members of the genus, its breeding habits depart from the norm (most

Some North American members of the genus *Hyla* are prized as pets. Photo by W. B. Allen, Jr.

The Pacific chorus frog, *Pseudacris regilla* occurs over much of the western U.S. coast, parts of Baja, and even into Canada. Photo by K. Lucas, Steinhart Aquarium.

hylids simply lay their eggs in bodies of water) in that a limited amount of parental care is shown. The eggs are laid in a specially prepared walled enclosure close to the edge of a still or slow-moving water course and are guarded until they hatch, when the larvae are released into the main body of water.

Hyla gratiosa, the barking tree frog, is a very attractive species from North America that makes a rewarding terrarium inmate. It is native to the coastal plain from southeastern Virginia to Florida and Louisiana. It inhabits the tree tops in the summer, but burrows into the ground in winter or during dry periods. It is mainly active at night. Growing to 6.5 cm (2.5 in), it has a short, almost pug-like head and snout and a very conspicuous ear-drum. The skin is granular and usually leaf-green, with dark gray to brown roundish blotches; in addition, small lemon-yellow spots are scattered over the upper side. The common name comes from the loud barking call, emitted by the male during rain. The mating call, however, is a single bell-like note. It requires a tall, planted terrarium with adequate ventilation and temperature in the region of 21-27°C (70-81°F), reduced to 17-20°C (63-68°F) in winter for a couple of months. Feed on a variety of small invertebrates.

Hyla pulchella is a small (5 cm, 2 in) species from southeastern Brazil, Uruguay, Bolivia, southern Paraguay, and northern Argentina that inhabits bush and forest land. It is slenderly built and has a relatively small mouth. The skin of the upper side is smooth or faintly granular and is usually plain green or marbled with darker green to brown. A white stripe extends from the corner of the mouth below the eye and along the flank to the thigh. The area below the stripe is darker than the back color. The underside is yellowish. It requires a tall, humid terrarium with adequate plant cover. Temperature 23-27°C (73-81°F). Feed on a variety of invertebrates.

Hyla regilla, the Pacific tree frog, is another species that is very much suited to the terrarium. Native to the western side of North America from British Columbia to Baja California and eastward to Montana, Idaho, and Nevada. Growing to a maximum of 5 cm (2 in), the male has a very pleasing two-toned call. It has a fairly rough, granular skin and is highly variable in color, ranging from green to light or dark brown with a range of darker patterns. The underside is usually uniform yellowish to grayish. Captive housing and care are similar to those described for *Hyla cinerea*. Recently this species has been transferred to the genus *Pseudacris* by some workers.

Osteopilus is a genus with three species, the one of interest to hobbyists being *O. septentrionalis*, the Cuban or giant tree frog, which was formerly included in the genus *Hyla* and is a very popular terrarium subject. Growing to a massive 14 cm (5.5 in), it is a relative giant when compared to other members of the family.

Unlike other chorus frogs, the ornate chorus Frog, *Pseudacris ornata*, is not a very good climber and spends almost all its life underground. Photo by R. T. Zappalorti.

It is native to Cuba and other West Indian islands and has been introduced successfully into Puerto Rico and southern Florida. The head is wide and the eyes relatively large. It has a very conspicuous tympanum. The skin is rough, and that covering the skull is fused with the bone. It has relatively large adhesive discs on the fingers and toes. The color is yellowish brown above, marbled with darker brown. The limbs are faintly banded. During the breeding period the male develops a bronze shimmer and large green patches, making him a very handsome frog. It inhabits moist and shady places, usually in trees and shrubs and often in gardens. It breeds during May to October in almost any body of water, including domestic cisterns and irrigation ditches. In captivity it requires a large, tall terrarium. In view of the weight of the frogs, only robust plants and climbing branches should be provided. Maintain the temperature in the range 25-29°C (77-84°F), reduced to 20-22°C (68-72°F) at night.

Pseudacris is a genus containing about a dozen species of chorus frogs, all native to North America. *P. ornata*, the ornate chorus frog, is native to the coastal plain extending from North Carolina to central Florida and eastern Louisiana. Growing to 3.5 cm (1.5 in), it is a plump little frog with relatively short limbs. Although a "tree frog," the adhesive finger and toe discs are barely developed. Indeed, these frogs are poor and unwilling climbers. The ground coloration of the upper suface is very variable, ranging from olive to gray and reddish brown. There is a broad, light-edged black stripe running from the snout and through the eye to the shoulder, usually breaking into blotches along the flank to the thigh. The limbs are banded in dark brown to black. The underside is a uniform off-white. *P. ornata* often spawn in flooded, grassy meadows. They require a shallow terrarium with medium humidity (except during the breeding season in January-February, when the humidity should be raised). Maintain the temperature at

This is a male little grass frog, *Pseudacris ocularis*, in the middle of a trill. Most chorus frog trills are very pleasant sounding. Photo by R. D. Bartlett.

16-22°C (60-72°F), reduced in the winter for a couple of months before the start of the breeding season. Other members of the genus include *P. clarki*, the spotted chorus frog; *P. nigrita*, the southern chorus frog; and *P. triseriata*, the common chorus frog, all requiring similar care. *Hyla crucifer* and *Hyla regilla* are in some respects intermediate between typical North American *Hyla* and *Pseudacris*, recently being assigned to the latter genus. *Hyla* in the broad sense is a very complex genus sure to be split in various ways in the future.

Smiliscus a genus containing about six species of treefrogs found from extreme southern Texas through Central America to northwestern South America. In most species, the female is larger than the male. In *S. baudinii* (Mexican treefrog), the female grows to 9 cm (3.75 in), the male to 7.5 cm (3 in). It is very variable in color, usually greenish to brownish with darker, elongate blotches. The flanks have dark spots on an off-white background that merges with the underside. This species estivates in hollow tree stumps, bromeliad tubes, or underground burrows during the dry season, but it will remain active with adequate humidity. It normally spawns in stagnant pools after abundant rain. In captivity it requires a tall terrarium with temperatures at 23-28°C (73-82°F), reduced somewhat for a period in the winter when the humidity can also be reduced. Increased humidity and temperature in the spring may induce breeding.

Subfamily Pelodryadinae

This subfamily of treefrogs contains three genera, all native to the Australo-Papuan region.

Litoria is a genus of over 100 species occurring in eastern Indonesia, Papua New Guinea, Solomon Islands, and in all parts of Australia including Tasmania. Many, but by no means all, are superficially similar to the typical hylid treefrogs (*Litoria* species were formerly included within *Hyla*, but along with with other Australian and New Guinea species were relegated to their own subfamily in 1977 and received a new generic name. The genus includes a number of species highly prized for the terrarium due to their size, color, and/or personality.

Perhaps the most famous species in the genus and one of the most popular all-time terrarium inmates is *L. caerulea*, White's treefrog (named after its first description in 1790 by J. White in his *Journal of a Voyage to New South Wales*). Its popularity is due to its tendency of being tame and

The genus *Litoria* is very large, containing well over 100 different species. Photo of *L. infrafrenata* by J. Wines.

trusting from the very first day it is taken into captivity. Reaching a length of approxsimately 10 cm (4 in), it is one of the larger members of the subfamily. It is also a very robust species that often gives the impression of being "overweight" due to its plumpness and the folds of flesh seen on older specimens. It has large finger and toe pads.

The color is predominently bluish green (all-blue specimens occasionally turn up), sometimes with a few small but vivid white spots scattered over the back. Its underside is usually a creamy or yellowish white.

It occurs in the eastern and northern parts of Australia and in southern New Guinea. Often encountered near human habitations, where it seeks out the moist areas associated with domestic water tanks, dams, and cisterns. It is mainly nocturnal and has a deep throaty croak. In captivity it should be provided with a large, tall terrarium with robust plants and solid branches on which it can climb. Keep the humidity moderate, with good ventilation and daytime temperatures to 30°C (86°F), but reduced to around 20°C (68°F) at night. Feed on a variety of larger invertebrates, including crickets, locusts, cockroaches, beetles, and moths. Requires a deep (not less than 30 cm, 12 in) pool if breeding is contemplated. Specimens may be brought into breeding condition by reducing temperature and humidity for a few weeks, then greatly increasing humidity over a period of several days. White's treefrog is bred in large numbers today and is one of the most available and cheapest of the terrarium frogs.

Nyctimystes is a genus with about 25 species native to the eastern Moluccas, New Guinea, and northern Queensland. It differs from *Litoria* in having a vertical rather than horizontal pupil. *N. humeralis*, at 10 cm (4 in), is the largest species in the genus. Found in the mountains of central New Guinea, this handsome treefrog is mainly bright green, with yellow blotches along the flanks. The underside is yellowish white. It requires a rainforest aquaterrarium with high humidity and temperatures of 25-30°C (77-86°F), reduced marginally at night. Feed on a variety of invertebrates. *N. tympanocryptis*, from northern Queensland, is beautifully marked in a marbling of olive and brown, interspersed with dark-bordered white botches. Requires care similar to that for *N. humeralis*.

Subfamily Phyllomedusinae

This subfamily contains three genera ranging from Mexico to Argentina.

Agalychnis is a group containing apprximately eight species ranging from southern Mexico to northern South America. Most are rather bizarre and make attractive

The red-eyed treefrog, _Agalychnis callidryas_, is undoubtedly one of the most unique and attractive frogs in the world. Photo by B. Kahl.

terrarium inmates for the advanced hobbyist. _A. callidryas_, the red-eyed treefrog of Central America, is, in the author's opinion, one of the most spectacular and colorful of all frogs. Reaching 7.5 cm (3 in) in length, it has a slender body and extraordinary matchstick-thin limbs. It is leaf green on the back, often sprinkled with a few white spots. The flanks are vertically banded in sky-blue and cream; the limbs are green above and blue below, while the feet and padded toes are a bright orange-red. Probably its most prominent feature is the pair of large, spectacular, crimson-red eyes with vertical pupils. It is a strictly arboreal and nocturnal frog of the tropical rain forest.

The red-eyed treefrog is a rather delicate captive and

should be considered only by experienced fanciers. It should be kept in a well-ventilated, tall terrarium with a high humidity produced preferably with moving water (an airlift-waterfall or drip system) or with regular mist spraying. Large-leaved plants such as *Philodendron* or *Monstera* species should be provided. Maintain at a temperature of 25-28°C (77-82°F), reduced to 20°C (68°F) at night. Feed on a variety of invertebrates, especially flies and moths. This species breeds in the foliage canopy. The eggs are laid on leaves overhanging a pool or stream, and the larvae drop into the water as they hatch a few days later. These develop in the normal way, leaving the water as fully developed little treefrogs after a few weeks. They require a large terrarium with a pool if captive breeding is to be accomplished. Other members of the genus, including *A. annae* of Costa Rica and *A. moreletti* of southern Mexico to Guatemala, require similar captive care.

Pachymedusa dacnicolor is the single species of a monotypic genus in the Pacific lowlands of Mexico. Growing to approximately 10 cm (4 in), it is an arboreal species, predominently green above and yellowish below, but its most spectacular feature is the large eyes with golden irides finely reticulated in black. This species requires similar care to *Agalychnis*, but with periods of lower humidity.

Phyllomedusa contains about 33 species from Central and South America. *P. lemur*, from Costa Rica and Panama, reaches a length of 6 cm (2.5 in). Its stature is similar to *Agalychnis*, and it is mainly green above, with a pink underside and orange groin. The outstanding feature of frogs of this genus is the very large eyes with vertical pupils and the opposable first finger and first toe enabling the frogs to "walk" in a monkey-like along narrow twigs. Habitat, breeding habits, and care are similar to *Agalychnis*. Other species in the genus requiring similar care include *P. fimbriata* from southeastern Brazil and *P. trinitatis* from Trinidad and northern Venezuela.

FAMILY HYPEROLIIDAE

This family was formerly considered by most herpetologists to be a subfamily of the Rhacophoridae, but it is now generally agreed that the Hyperoliidae is a family in its own right. The hyperolids consist of three subfamilies, 13 genera, and some 220 species found mostly in Africa, with a few species in Madagascar and the Seychelles. The best known members of the family are the reed frogs of the genus *Hyperolius*, of which there are 118 species spread over most of Africa south of the Sahara.

This close relative of the red-eyed treefrog, known as *A. annae*, hails from Costa Rica. Photo by G. Dibley.

The reed frogs of the genus *Hyperolius* are found over much of Africa and vary greatly in both color and pattern. Photo by K. Lucas, Steinhart Aquarium.

Hyperolius contains some 120 species native to Africa south of the Sahara, many of them are very similar and posing difficult taxonomic problems. All are small frogs with adhesive discs on their toes for climbing. The males have a chirping call and a single large vocal sac. Perhaps the most abundant species is *H. marmoratus*, the marbled reed frog, which occurs in central, eastern and southern Africa and is a particularly "difficult" species taxonomically, with over 20 supposedly distinctive races described. The colors are highly variable through greens, browns, and yellows and it may be marbled, blotched, striped, or spotted. Growing to about 4 cm (1.5 in), reed frogs live mainly in vegetation close to marshes, rivers and ponds. During dry periods they estivate in the mud. Active by day or night, some are fond of "sun bathing" on cool mornings.

Reed frogs require a tall terrarium with sturdy grasses

Most members of the very interesting genus *Kassina* walk or run more often than they hop. Photo by K. Lucas, Steinhart Aquarium.

or, preferably, semiaquatic plants growing in shallow, warm water. A high humidity and temperatures of 22-28°C (72-82°F) should be maintained. Feed on a variety of small invertebrates. The species have varied breeding habits. *H. marmoratus* lays its small batches of eggs on the upper side of submerged plants, so a planted aquaterrarium will be necessary for captive breeding.

Kassina is a genus containing about 12 species of "running frogs," so-called due to their habit of running or walking rather than hopping. Most are attractively colored and make good terrarium subjects. They are nocturnal and terrestrial, estivating during dry periods in mud burrows and breeding in surface waters after heavy rains. A typical species is *K. cassinoides* from the dry savannahs of West Africa. Reaching 4.5 cm (1.75 in), the ground color is silvery gray, marked with black blotches and/or stripes. *K. maculata* from East Africa grows to 6.5 cm (2.5 in) and is light gray with light-edged oval black blotches. Perhaps the best known of the species is the Senegal running frog, *K. senegalensis*, which is not, however, restricted to Senegal, being extremely common and abundant in the entire savannah regions of tropical Africa. An attractive little frog growing to 4 cm (1.5 in), this species is highly variable in color and pattern, but most patterns are based on dark longitudinal stripes on a lighter background.

Kassina species require a small, tropical terrarium with a few suitable plants. High humidity should be maintained when breeding is required, otherwise keep moderately humid. A temperature of around 26°C (79°F) is recommended. Feed on a variety of small invertebrates.

FAMILY LEIOPELMATIDAE

A small but interesting family containing two genera, one with a single species in North America and the other with three species in New Zealand. There is some argument for the fact that the two genera should be allocated to separate families. They often are considered to be the most primitive of all living frogs. One unique aspect of the family is that tail-wagging muscles (caudaliopuboischiotibialis !) are retained in the adult.

Ascaphus is a monotypic genus containing the so called "tailed" frog, *A. truei*, which ranges from southern British Columbia south to northwestern California, with separate inland populations in Montana and Idaho. Although no frog has a true tail as such, the male of this species has a unique tail-like extension of the vent which is used as a copulatory organ to introduce sperm directly into the body of the female. *A. truei* is a squat, somewhat flattened frog that grows to 5 cm (2 in) in length. It has small warts and tubercles on the skin and usually is olive to gray or black, with many irregular dark blotches on the back. A dark stripe runs from the snout through the eye, and there is a small yellowish patch on top of the head. The pupil is vertical. There is no vocal sac

An attractive example of the South American frog *Physalaemus nattereri*. Photo by I. Sazima.

in the male, which therefore has no voice.

It is mainly aquatic, inhabiting cool, clear mountain streams, but may be occasionally found out of the water in damp, shady areas. It breeds from May to September, attaching its eggs to the downstream side of rocks. The tadpoles are equipped with sucking mouthparts to enable them to cling to solid surfaces in strong currents. The larvae feed on algae and small invertebrates; development and metamorphosis may take two or more years. In captivity, the frogs should be kept in an aquaterrarium with more water than land. The water should be maintained at 10-12°C (50-54°F) and should be filtered and agitated. Some large stones should be placed in the substrate. Breeding response may be triggered by an increase in photoperiod and very slight (1-2°C) increase in temperature. Feed on small aquatic invertebrates.

Leiopelma is a genus of three species native to New Zealand (where they are strictly protected) and the only living amphibians native to that country other than introductions. There is no tympanic membrane, a method of distinguishing New Zealand's native frogs from introduced species. *Leiopelma* species do not have a free-swimming tadpole stage—the early stages of development take place inside a gelatinous capsule surrounding the egg. A tiny, tailed froglet eventually emerges from the capsule. The most common of the three species is *L. hochstetteri*, a plump-bodied frog growing to 4.5 cm (1.75 in). The skin is granular, with glandular ridges and warts scattered over the upper body. The color is variable, but usually is very dark brown above, lighter beneath. There are darker bands across the thighs. This species is found in the northern part of the North Island of New Zealand, where it inhabits damp situations close to water. Though unlikely to find their way into many terraria at the present time, captive-bred specimens may eventually be available. They

The Argentine horned frog, *Ceratophrys ornata*, has fast become one of the most commonly-kept frogs of all time. Photo of a female by C. Alt.

FAMILY LEPTODACTYLIDAE

This New World family contains four subfamilies and well over 700 species occurring from the southern USA to southern South America, and including the West Indian islands. The family has been under constant revision and further changes are likely.

Ceratophrys contains the horned frogs. No book about amphibians should fail to mention this genus, which contains six species called escuerzos in their native South America. All of them are most spectacular and are highly popular terrarium subjects. *Ceratophrys ornata*, the ornate horned frog, shows a remarkable similarity in appearance and habits to the unrelated African bullfrog, *Pyxicephalus adspersus*. Like other members of the genus, it has a large head and a huge gape. There is a fleshy "horn" over each eye, and the hind limbs are relatively short. It has bony, tooth-like projections in the lower jaw and is capable of giving a painful bite. The colors are highly variable but usually

will require a humid terrarium with temperatures not greater than 22°C (72°F), reduced somewhat in the winter. The other two species in the genus are *L. archeyi*, from the Coromandel Peninsula in the North Island, and *L. hamiltoni*, from very restricted localities on Stephens Island and Maud Island off the northern tip of the South Island.

consist of greens, reddish browns, and creams. Growing to a length of 17.5 cm (7 in), this species is found in the pampas regions of Argentina, Uruguay, and Brazil.

During excessively dry periods it spends much of its time holed up in a burrow and is brought into activity and breeding condition by seasonal rains. It is a remarkably powerful, fearless frog that can overpower and swallow creatures almost its own size, including small mammals, birds, reptiles, and other frogs. It may lie in ambush in a shallow burrow with only the top of the head exposed. It requires a terrarium with medium humidity, a deep substrate, and a water dish for bathing. Daytime temperatures should be about 27°C (81°F), reduced by a few degrees at night. Feed on a variety of large invertebrates, including earthworms and snails. Only specimens of similar size should be kept together; on no account keep larger and smaller specimens, together otherwise you are likely to end up with only larger ones; in severe cases you may end up with just one very large specimen! (On second thought, perhaps it is best to keep every specimen in its own terrarium and play safe.) Related species such as C. *aurita* from southeastern Brazil and *C. cornuta* from northeastern Brazil and the Guianas have similar habits and require similar husbandry.

Lepidobatrachus is a genus containing just three species, which are closely related to *Ceratophrys* and have similar habits, though they are somewhat plainer in color. The tadpoles of frogs in this genus are carnivorous and remarkably aggressive. Care is similar to that for *Ceratophrys*.

Leptodactylus, with about 50 species, is the largest and most important genus in the subfamily. The larger species are said to be the neotropical equivalents of *Rana* (virtually absent from the neotropics), to which many are superficially similar. Most are found at low altitudes (less than 1200 meters, 3900 ft), where they are usually in the vicinity of water. Species from drier areas estivate in burrows or beneath ground litter until brought into

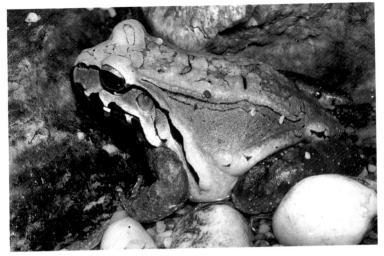

Commonly called the South American bullfrog, *Leptodactylus pentadactylus* is one of the larger species of its genus. Photo by K. Lucas, Steinhart Aquarium.

activity by rains. Most species are foam nest builders, the nest being made in the water itself or in specially excavated pools in the mud near the main water body. Some build a mud wall around the pool, and others even cover it over with (probably as a protection against desiccation). Hatchling larvae wriggle their own way to the main body of water after heavy rainfall.

Leptodactylus fragilis (usually called *L. labialis* in U.S. field guides), the white-lipped frog, occurs from extreme southern Texas through Mexico to Panama. Measuring up to 5 cm (2 in) in length, it is grayish to brownish with irregular dark blotches on the back and stripes across the thighs. There is a conspicuous white line along the upper lip. It has prominent dorsolateral folds. Hiding in burrows during the day, it comes out to forage at night. It breeds in May and June after heavy rain and manufactures a foam nest, often placed in a rain-filled depression that is scooped out by the male. It requires a large aquaterrarium with facilities for burrowing. Temperature should be maintained around 25°C (77°F), reduced a little at night.

Leptodactylus pentadactylus is one of the larger species, growing to a massive 20 cm (8 in). It is commonly called the South American bullfrog due to its size and is found from Honduras south to Peru and northern Brazil. A semiaquatic species that is highly variable in color though usually shades of brown on the back and reddish brown on the flanks. It requires a large aquaterrarium with rather more water than land. Maintain the temperature at 25-28°C (77-82°F). Feed on large invertebrates and small vertebrates (pink mice, small fish). Do not keep large and small specimens together as they are likely to be cannibalistic.

Pleurodema is a genus of toad-like leptodactylids with about 12 species native to most parts of South America, but with some species from high in the Andes (to 4500 m, 14,500 ft) and from the far south. Most

The single species of its genus, *Caudiverbera caudiverbera* hails from central Chile and only moves about during the night. Photo by R. D. Bartlett.

species walk rather than jump and estivate or hibernate in burrows during unsuitable weather. *P. bibroni*, from southern Brazil and Uruguay, reaches 5 cm (2 in). It is grayish brown with darker marbling and has large "eye"

This species requires an unheated terrarium and may even be suited to an outdoor enclosure in temperate climates.

Caudiverbera is a monotypic genus containing the species *C. caudiverbera* from central Chile. It is a large (to 23 cm, 9 in), robust, toad-like animal with a warty skin. Its color is olive-brown with lighter blotches. Nocturnal and semiaquatic, it spend its daylight hours buried on land. It requires a large, unheated aquaterrarium with facilities to burrow in the land portion. It feeds in the water, and will take fish and small mice as well as large invertebrates.

Eleutherodactylus is the largest amphibian genus, with over 420 species described and more being described on a regular basis. They occur from Mexico through Central America and the West Indies to southern Brazil and northern Argentina, where they occur in a great variety of habitats from sea level to altitudes of 4000 meters (13000 ft). Most are nocturnal, hiding under cover during the day. There is no aquatic larval

markings on its lower back. When threatened, it raises its back by extending its hind legs and presenting its large "eyes" in the hope of deterring a predator. *P. bufonia* is native to the grasslands of Patagonian Argentina and southern Chile and, as such, is distinguished as the world's most southerly amphibian. Reaching 5 cm (2 in) in length, it is light gray in color with large black blotches.

stage. Eggs are laid in damp situations on land. After two to three weeks, fully metamorphosed froglets emerge. Most require a small planted, humid terrarium with temperatures reflecting the native habitat of the individual species.

Eleutherodactylus coqui (5 cm, 2 in) is native to Puerto Rico and is introduced into Louisiana and Florida. It is grayish brown with a broad light stripe down either side of the back; the male has a two-toned bird-like chirp. *E. diadematus* (4.5 cm, 1.75 in) from Amazonian Ecuador and Peru atypically lives in the foliage of trees and shrubs and deposits its eggs in bromeliad cups. It is light fawn in color with dark brown or black markings. *E. johnstonei* (2 cm, 0.75 in) a tiny terrestrial frog from the Lesser Antilles and also introduced into Jamaica, is reddish brown with darker markings on its back. The male has an attractive whistling call. *E. planirostris*, from the West Indies and very successfully introduced into Florida, measures up to 3 cm (1.25 in) and is reddish brown with

either dark mottling or light dorsolateral stripes.

Hylactophryne is a genus containing three species found from the southwestern USA to southern Mexico. This genus often is considered part of *Eleutherodactylus*. *H. augusti*, commonly known as the barking frog because the male's call is similar to a dog's bark, is found in an arc from southeastern New Mexico and central Texas into Mexico and returning to southern Arizona. It grows to 10 cm (4 in) and is a robust species with a relatively large head and forward-oriented eyes. It has a smooth skin and is greenish to brownish with scattered dark spots. There is a disc-shaped skin fold on its belly. It is a nocturnal and mainly terrestrial species, though it may climb rock surfaces. When threatened it can inflate its body to many times its normal size. It inhabits damp limestone caves and similar locations and breeds from February to May after sufficiently heavy rains. The eggs are laid in moist situations on land, and full metamorphosis takes place in the egg. In captivity it requires a semi-humid terrarium with a gravel and rock substrate and a few potted plants. Increase moisture in spring to induce spawning.

Syrrhophus contains 15 species ranging from southern Texas to Guatemala. Closely related to and superficially similar to *Eleutherodactylus* species, all are nocturnal and terrestrial, laying their eggs in damp situations on land. There is no aquatic larval stage, full metamorphosis taking place within the egg. They require a semi-humid planted terrarium with adequate hiding places. *S. cystignathoides*, the Rio Grande chirping frog, comes from extreme southern Texas and eastern Mexico. A tiny frog reaching just 2.5 cm (1 in) and often smaller, it has truncated digits, these being more prominent on the fingers than the toes. It is grayish to yellow with darker blotching on a finely granular skin. Often it is found in well-watered gardens and plantations. *S. guttilatus*, the spotted chirping frog, occurs in southern central Texas and south into Mexico. It reaches 3.3 cm (1.25 in) and is yellowish brown with dark

This is the Lake Titicaca Frog, *Telmatobius culeus*. Photo by A. Norman.

undulating lines on a smooth skin. It lives mainly near springs and in moist caves. As the common names imply, the males of these frogs have a chirping call somewhat similar to that of a cricket.

Telmatobius is a genus containing over 30 species native to the Andean region of South America between altitudes of 2000 and 4500 m

(6500 to 14500 ft). Most are fully aquatic, living in streams, rivers, or lakes. They are oval in shape and usually fairly plainly colored. They require a roomy, cool, aquarium (8-15°C, 46-59°F is adequate) decorated with piles of large pebbles, one or two of which should reach the surface. They feed on aquatic invertebrates, tadpoles, small fish (guppies), etc. *T. culeus* reaches 12.5 cm (5 in) and are from Lake Titicaca and surrounding areas of Peru and Bolivia. *T. marmoratus*, to 6 cm (2.5 in), is from the same region.

FAMILY MICROHYLIDAE

This family has a number of taxonomic problems, but here we recognize nine subfamilies distributed almost worldwide, including North and South America, sub-Saharan Africa, India, Southeast Asia, and northern Australia. Many are commonly known as narrow-mouthed frogs due to the usually somewhat rotund shape, small head, and narrow gape.

Breviceps is a genus containing 12 species from southern Africa, where they inhabit semi-desert, savannah, and woodland. They have an almost spherical body with a small head and short limbs. They are terrestrial, burrowing frogs that spend dry periods below ground, emerging to feed and breed after heavy rains. Food is mainly ants and termites. As far as is known, all *Breviceps* species lay their eggs in a specially dug chamber from which fully or almost fully developed froglets eventually hatch. In captivity they require a terrarium with burrowing facilities and temperatures in the range of 22-30°C (72-86°F). Artificially produced wet and dry seasons should be provided to help them behave as naturally as possible. *B. adspersus*, from Namibia, Botswana, Zimbabwe, Mozambique, and northern South Africa, grows to 5 cm (2 in). It is usually yellowish-orange on the base with dark brown and with a dark vertebral stripe. *B. verrucosus*, from the Eastern Plateau slopes, South Africa, and Lesotho, measures up to 7.5 cm (3 in) and is usually light brown with a reticulated pattern of dark brown. The

Right: One of the most "famous" of all frogs is without a doubt the tomato frog, *Dyscophus antongilli*. Photo by K. H. Switak.

Below: The eastern narrowmouth toad, *Gastrophryne carolinensis*, occurs only in the eastern United States. Photo by R. T. Zappalorti.

closely related genus *Probreviceps*, with three species, has similar habits and requires similar care.

Dyscophus is a genus containing three species from Madagascar, including the famous tomato frog, *D. antongilii*, which is a prized terrarium exhibit if it can be obtained. It is a relatively large (female 11 cm, 4.5 in; male 7.5 cm, 3 in) frog, and bright tomato red in color. It inhabits ditches and streams in the coastal regions of northeastern Madagascar, thus it requires a humid, planted aquaterrarium with temperatures of 25-30°C (77-86°F). It feeds on medium to large invertebrates, and has recently has been bred in captivity, becoming more generally available, although captive-breds may be paler in color than wild-caught specimens.

Gastrophryne is a genus containing about six species known as narrowmouthed frogs (or toads), occurring from the southern United States to Costa Rica. *G. carolinensis*, the eastern narrowmouth toad, occurs in the southeastern USA, where it is normally found among moist debris near water. It reaches 4 cm (1.5 in) in length and has an egg-shaped body, a pointed snout, and a fold of skin across the back of the head. Color is variable, from dark gray to reddish brown, usually with lighter stripes along the flanks. It breeds from April to October, the eggs being laid in a floating sheet. Terrestrial and burrowing, it seems to prefer ants as its main food source. Keep in a humid aqua-terrarium with temperatures in the range of 21-26°C (70-79°F). *G. olivacea*, the closely related Great Plains narrowmouth toad, occurs from Nebraska to Texas and into Mexico, and requires similar husbandry but with less humidity (except when a breeding response is required).

Hypopachus contains two species occurring from the southern United States to Costa Rica. *H. variolosus*, the sheep frog (named for the male's bleating call), occurs from southeastern Texas to Costa Rica. Reaching 4.5 cm (1.75 in), it has smooth skin and a pointed snout. There is a fold of skin across the back of the head. It is brown to olive on the back, with black spots and a light yellow vertebral stripe. The flanks are grayish, and there is a cream patch below the eye. Feeding largely on ants and termites, it spends the day concealed in a burrow or under debris. It breeds after adequate rains make temporary pools. In captivity it requires a terrarium with facilities for burrowing and artificial wet/dry seasons.

Kaloula is a genus containing nine species native to eastern and Southeast Asia. The best-known species is *K. pulchra*, the Malayan narrowmouth toad, also known as the Indian Bull or ox frog, so named after its call, which resembles the bellowing of an

Here are two beautiful *Phrynomerus annectans*, one juvenile and the other an adult. Photo by P. Freed.

ox. This widespread species occurs from Sri Lanka and southern India to southern China, Malaysia, and the Celebes. Growing to 7.5 cm (3 in), it is a robust frog with short but powerful limbs. The ground color is dark chocolate brown above, with a broad, irregularly edged pale (mustard yellow to pink or reddish) band extending along the sides and joining across the front of the head. The underside is mottled dark and light brown. It has horny "spades" on the feet which are used for burrowing. This is a less secretive frog than most in the family and, although nocturnal and burrowing, it often turns up near human habitations, occasionally joining the toads under street or porch lights to catch falling insects. It will feed on ants and termites as well as the usual food insects, and breeds at any time of the year after adequate rain in temporary static waters. Eggs appear as large sheets floating on the water surface. Metamorphosis takes place in as little as 14 days from oviposition. In captivity they require a semi-humid terrarium with artificial wet/dry periods. Feed on a variety of small invertebrates.

Phrynomerus contains four species native to sub-Saharan Africa, most in semi-arid or arid areas. They have a depressed body with a small head. The pupil is vertical and the eardrum is not externally visible. The hind limbs are very short. They are nocturnal and terrestrial, moving with a walk, being unable to jump. During the day, and in unsuitable weather conditions, they remain in their self-excavated burrows. In captivity they require a terrarium with burrowing facilities and wet/dry seasons. *P. annectens*, found from Angola to Cape Province, grows to 3.5 cm (1.5 in). It is grayish to dark brown with round green, black, and reddish brown spots. *P. bifasciatus*, with several subspecies, ranges from Somalia to South Africa. Reaching 5.5 cm (2.25 in), it is blackish brown with a cream to orange stripe down each side of the back and spots of the same color on the flanks and limbs.

FAMILY MYOBATRACHIDAE

This rather controversial family contains two subfamilies of frogs, all native to Australia and New Guinea. Until recently, they were regarded as a subfamily of the family

The ornate burrowing frog, ***Limnodynastes ornatus*, varies highly in both color and pattern. Photo by J. Coborn.**

Leptodactylidae.
    Limnodynastes is a genus containing 12 species of robust terrestrial and/or burrowing frogs that build a floating foam nest. *L. ornatus*, the ornate burrowing frog, occurs in eastern and northern Australia. Reaching 4.5 cm (1.8 in) in length, it is very variable in color and pattern, ranging from almost uniform dark brown to

pale gray or fawn with numerous lighter or darker markings. There is sometimes a light yellow or orange dorsal stripe. The underside is white. It occurs in a wide range of habitats from rainforest to dry woodlands and it is active after summer rains, when it may be seen abroad at night.

In order to keep the northern banjo frog, *Limnodynastes terraereginae*, you will need a semi-dry terrarium with plenty of soft burrowing material. Photo by J. Coborn.

Limnodynastes terrareginae, the northern banjo frog, is a spectacular species measuring up to 7.5 cm (3 in) in length. It is usually reddish brown with obscure darker flecks and blotches. There is a broad black band extending from the eye to the arm, bordered above with a narrow cream stripe and below by a broader reddish stripe. The flanks are orange-red with black marbling, running into bright crimson in the groin and with similar bright crimson spots on the back of the thighs. It has similar habits to *L. ornatus*. *L. tasmaniensis*, from south and eastern Australia, is not so much a burrower, being found under ground litter during the day. All species in the genus require a semi-dry terrarium with facilities to burrow or hide and artificial wet seasons to encourage breeding.

Notaden is a genus containing three species, including the well-known *N. bennettii*, the holy-cross or crucifix toad from the plains of New South Wales and southern Queensland. Measuring up to 5 cm (2 in), the body is more or less globular and the limbs stubby. The skin is warty in texture. Color is olive, green, or yellow above, with low roundish black or dark brown warts and scattered red, yellow, and white spots arranged in the pattern of a crucifix. It is a burrowing species usually found on the surface only after rain. It breeds in temporary pools and requires a small terrarium with a deep, sandy substrate. Keep the cage dry in winter at a temperature of 15-20°C (59-68°F). A gradual increase in temperature (to 28°C, 82°F), the humidity, and provision of a pool may encourage a breeding response. Feed them on a variety of small invertebrates, including ants and termites.

Crinia has 14 species native to Australia and New Guinea. *Crinia signifera* is the common eastern froglet of southeastern Australia. It is a small (2.5 cm, 1 in) terrestrial frog, highly variable in color, through grays, browns, and fawns with stripes, bands, or blotches. It is very common in its range, occurring in almost every habitat and breeding in ditches, dams, puddles, cart ruts, etc., and requires a small aquaterrarium with a summer temperature range of 22-28°C (72-82°F), reduced for the winter rest period.

Pseudophryne is a genus of 11 species included here for the sake of the highly colorful *P. corroboree* from the mountains of southeastern New South Wales and the Australian Capital Territory. A small (3 cm, 1.25 in) frog, it is bright yellow above, and marked with many longitudinal black enamel-like stripes. It is found above the tree line in swampy grasslands or near streams in wet woodlands. A protected species that is unlikely to be available to the terrarium keeper unless captive breeding programs are implemented, it remains one of the best-known Australian frogs.

FAMILY PELOBATIDAE

This family contains two subfamilies with species through North America, southern and Southeast Asia to the Philippines, Europe, and North Africa.

Megophrys is a genus with some 22 species, one of which, the Asian horned frog, *M.*

montana, is common in the hobby, though better known by the name *M. nasuta*, which is either a synonym or subspecies depending on which reference you consult. It is a bizarre animal native to the forests of Thailand, Malaya, and Indonesia to Borneo and the Philippines. Recognized by a fleshy "horn" above each eye and another on the tip of the snout, its color is a mixture of browns and grays that provides good camouflage in its habitat. This species lives in the forest and spends the greater part of the day buried in leaf litter with just the highly camouflaged top of the head (resembling dead leaves) showing so that it can lunge at any passing prey. It should be housed in a tropical aquaterrarium with a land/water ratio of 2:1. The land area should be provided with a deep layer of leaf litter in which the frogs will hide. The leaf litter must be replaced at regular intervals as the humid atmosphere required will rapidly aid rotting. A few tropical plants will help maintain the humidity. Fairly constant but relatively cool

The southern spadefoot, *Pelobates cultripes*, is found in both southern France and along the Iberian Peninsula. Photo by G. Baumgart, courtesy Dr. D. Terver, Nancy Aquarium, France.

(24-26°C, 75-79°F) temperatures may be maintained all year. Feed on a variety of invertebrates.

Pelobates is a genus containing four species, the best known being the common Eurasian spadefoot, *P. fuscus*, sometimes referred to as the "garlic toad" due to its smell resembling that of the herb. It is found in lowland western, central, and eastern Europe, extending into Asia as far as southern Siberia and the northern Caucasus. This is a plump, toad-like anuran with prominent eyes and vertical pupils. Growing to about 8 cm (3.25 in), it is mainly buff in color, marked with blotches and stripes of light brown. It requires similar housing to *Scaphiopus*, but with cooler temperatures and greater (but not waterlogged!) humidity. In southern France and the Iberian peninsula it is replaced by the southern spadefoot, *P. cultripes*. *P. syriacus* from the Middle East and *P. varaldii* from North Africa require dryer conditions.

Scaphiopus is a genus containing six species all native to North America (including northern Mexico). *S. couchi* reaches 9 cm (3.5 in) in length and is a plump little toad with a relatively long, sickle-shaped spade on each foot. The fairly smooth skin has many tiny

A closeup of the parsley frog, *Pelodytes punctatus*, showing facial and back features. Photo by G. Baumgart, courtesy Dr. D. Terver, Nancy Aquarium, France.

pale tubercles. The color above, is bright greenish-yellow to brown with darker marbling. The underside is predominantly off-white. It occurs from southeastern California to southwestern Oklahoma and south into Mexico, where it prefers short grass prairie. It is quite tolerant of arid conditions but will estivate in a deep burrow during excessively dry periods. In more humid periods it emerges each night to hunt for its insect prey, burrowing again before it is endangered by the harsh rays of the daytime sun. It requires a terrarium with a deep, loose substrate (coarse sand). Provide a dish of water, but keep the substrate itself reasonably dry. The daytime air temperature can be as high as 30°C (86°F) and humidity can be low. Reduce the temperature at night to around 20°C (58°F). Reduce the temperature in winter to 10°C (50°F) for a couple of months of simulated hibernation. In the wild, breeding occurs after heavy rain and flash flooding and metamorphosis may occur in as little as two weeks. There are five more species found in the USA and Mexico, all requiring similar care.

FAMILY PELODYTIDAE

This family contains but a single genus and just two species. It has been considered by some herpetologists to be a subfamily (Pelodytinae) of the Pelobatidae, but unlike this family, they are always small and slender and do not possess "spades."

Pelodytes punctatus, the parsley frog, occurs in southwestern Europe below a line drawn from the central Belgian coast to northwestern Italy. It is rarely more than 5 cm (2 in) and is a long-limbed, agile frog with a flattened head and relatively large eyes. The pupils are vertical. The skin above is fairly warty and usually pale grayish to light olive, sprinkled with small "parsley green" spots. The warts along the flanks may be orange. Like *P. fuscus*, this species often has a garlic-like smell. It breeds in spring and summer in deep, still, vegetated waters. Outside the breeding season it hides during the day under ground litter, but becomes active at night. It requires an unheated aquaterrarium with hiding places on the land portion. *P. caucasicus*, from the Caucasus and neighboring parts of the Russian nations and Turkey, is similar in appearance and habits and requires similar care.

FAMILY PIPIDAE

The Pipidae is a relatively small family of highly aquatic anurans with interesting habits and includes some with most unusual breeding habits. As such, they are very popular with aquarium keepers who like to keep something "different." The Pipidae is divided into two subfamilies.

Subfamily Pipinae

A single genus and seven species inhabiting tropical America.

Pipa includes the Surinam toad, *P. pipa*, which must be one of the most bizarre looking and interesting of all anurans and, as such, is a very popular animal with herp keepers. It is one of seven species in the subfamily Pipinae, all of which are totally aquatic and native to the northern parts of South America, one reaching as far north as Panama (*P. myersi*). *P. pipa* inhabits slow-moving watercourses from Colombia to Bolivia, Peru, and Ecuador and from the Guianas to parts

A mating pair of *Pipa pipa*. Photo by K. Lucas, Steinhart Aquarium.

of Brazil, Venezuela, and Trinidad. Reaching up to 20 cm (8 in) in length, the Surinam toad has a flattened body and a pointed snout. Its front limbs are relatively small, and the unwebbed fingers are furnished at the tips with very sensitive, star-like appendages that are used to locate food items in murky waters. The hind limbs are large and powerful, and the huge feet are provided with long, completely webbed toes. The eyes are relatively small and, as in all pipids, are situated on top of the head. The color is a rather drab mixture of grays and browns above and dusky white below. It is mainly active at night, spending most of the day quietly resting on the substrate, preferably in a shadowed spot. It has the appearance of being a rather sluggish creature but can move remarkably fast when it comes up for air, when feeding, or when alarmed.

A pair may be kept in an aquarium with a capacity of not less than 150 liters (about 35 gallons) and a water depth of not less than 30 cm (12 in). The substrate should consist of a rather coarse gravel. Only robust plants, if any, should be used. For most of the year, the temperature can be maintained at around 26°C (70°F). An aquarium filter and some kind of recirculatory system are considered essential for these anurans. A jugful of water should be exchanged each day. Feed the toads on live fishes (guppies, for example), strips of lean meat (beef, chicken, or ox heart), earthworms, and similar fare.

Perhaps the most interesting aspect of the Surinam toad is its breeding habits. In the wild state, the animals are induced to breed by the onset of heavy rains that may follow a period of drought. In captivity this phenomenon can be artificially reproduced by gradually reducing the water level over a period of two to three weeks until it is just 10 cm (4 in) in depth. Then, one day, the water is suddenly returned to not less than 30 cm (12 in) in depth, with a reduction in temperature to about 20°C (68°F), allowed to return slowly to 26°C (79°F) over a period of 24 hours. This should induce the toads to breed. First the male will emit his strange, metallic sounding "click-click-click," often for several hours, before grasping the female around the hips. While in amplexus, the pair performs a series of "somersaults," and each time the water surface is reached (in an upside-down position) the female releases a small number of eggs (usually 3-6) through her long ovipositor. The eggs are fertilized by the male, who then guides them onto the female's back which, by this time, will have become quite spongy. Some of the eggs may fall to the substrate, but these will be wasted and should preferably be removed with a pipette (after spawning is over). After performing several somersaults, often over a period of several hours, and having laid 40-100 eggs, the pair separates. The eggs adhere to the female's back, and in the next 24 hours the skin will begin to swell around the eggs until each one has its own individual chamber. Complete development of the larvae and metamorphosis occurs in each of these little nursery chambers. In 12-20 weeks, tiny but perfectly formed Surinam toads will emerge. These should be removed to a rearing tank and raised on tiny aquatic invertebrates or ground lean meat in very small quantities (beware of water pollution).

Subfamily Xenopodinae

Contains three genera of aquatic frogs, all native to sub-Saharan Africa.

Hymenochirus is a genus containing four species native to the equatorial areas of Africa. *H. boettgeri* is probably the best known. Native to the rainforest areas of central and western Africa, this little frog reaches a maximum length of 3.5 cm (1.5 in). It has a fairly rough skin and the body is dorsoventrally flattened. The head is relatively small and the snout is pointed; there are no eyelids. The dorsal surface is grayish brown with marbling of a darker color; the underside is a uniform grayish to yellowish white. The toes and fingers are webbed.

This almost totally aquatic species can be kept in similar conditions to *Xenopus*, although a smaller tank may be used. The water should also be shallower, and the temperature maintained at about 23°C (73°F). The dwarf clawed frog may be fed on a similar diet, though the respective food items should be relatively smaller. *H. boettgeri* can often be induced to breed by raising the ambient temperature by 4-5°C to about 27-28°C (81-82°F). Mating behavior shows many similarities to that of *Pipa*. The male grasps the female around the waist and both then rise to the surface, turning over onto

In 1983, this *Xenopus laevis* took 1st Place at the annual F.T.F.F.A. dealer show in Florida. Photo by Dr. H. Grier.

their backs as they do so. The male pumps at the female, who lays about 10-20 tiny eggs at a time that are simultaneously fertilized by the male sperm. The pair sink to the substrate and the process is repeated until as many as 1000 eggs are laid and fertilized. Eggs may be removed with a pipette and placed in a container of clean aerated water, which should be maintained at about 25°C (77°F). They should hatch in about three days, and in another three days the larvae will become free-swimming and seek food. The larvae of *Hymenochirus* are carnivorous and start feeding on tiny microorganisms. Infusoria or a jarful of stagnant pond-water should be added to the rearing tank at regular intervals—beware that no tadpole predators are introduced! As they grow they will take copepods, water fleas, and finely chopped tubifex worms. Other members of the genus require similar husbandry.

Xenopus is a genus containing about 14 species occurring in many parts of sub-Saharan Africa. *X. laevis*, the common clawed toad (or frog), is one of the most well-known and popular of the aquatic frogs, being used both in medical laboratories and as a pet. It is frequently bred in captivity and is often for sale in pet shops. It was this species that was used in pioneer pregnancy testing in women; the chorionic hormone produced by a pregnant woman causes the frogs to ovulate. The clawed frog reaches about 12.5 cm (5 in) in length and is powerfully built, with strong hind limbs and large feet with webbed toes, well adapted for swimming. The toes are armed with sharp "claws" that give the animal its common name. As claws are an unusual feature in anurans, the scientific name *Xenopus*, which is derived from the Greek, literally means "strange foot."

Xenopus has a very smooth, slippery skin, which makes it it quite difficult to hold in the hand, so it is therefore usually manipulated in a net. The normal color is gray to brown on the dorsal surface, marbled with darker shades. The underside is creamy white. Color mutations, including albinos, "goldens," and pieds are available. The small eyes are set on top of the head. Females are somewhat larger than the males and can be recognized by the three lobes or appendages arranged around the cloaca.

In its natural biotope, *Xenopus* lives in slow-moving streams and ponds in the savannah regions of eastern and southern Africa. During the dry season the adults are able to estivate in the thick muddy substrate of the water courses. New rains and flooding encourage it to breed. Although it prefers to remain aquatic, the clawed frog is able to move over land to new ponds during wet weather.

In captivity, a pair of clawed frogs can be comfortably housed in an aquarium 60 cm long by 30 cm deep by 40 cm wide (24 x 12 x 16 in). Provide a gravel substrate and

**Many African clawed frogs,
Xenopus laevis, are sold in
albino form, unlike the
normally colored one shown
here. Photo by K. Lucas,
Steinhart Aquarium.**

(preferably) a mechanical filter.
Maintain at a temperature of
22-27°C (72-81°F). The water
should be 15-20 cm (6-8 in)
deep, or just deep enough for
the frogs to break the surface
with the snout while the toes
are touching the substrate.
Floating plants and rocks may
be added for decoration. Plants
in the substrate will usually be
uprooted by the frogs in the
search for food unless you have
very well established plants in a
very large container. *Xenopus*
frogs can be kept in outdoor
pools in subtropical to tropical
climates or even in milder
temperate areas, but care
should be taken to prevent
escape of this species into the
wild, as it can have a
devastating effect on local
ecology. It has become a
successful colonist in southern
California and is, in fact,
prohibited in parts of the
western United States for this
very reason.

Xenopus may be fed on small
strips of lean raw meat,
especially beefsteak, ox-heart,
or chicken. Earthworms are

taken readily as well as the more common invertebrate foods. When meat must be given over long periods, a multivitamin/mineral supplement should be rubbed into it. Laboratory stock are often fed on specially formulated pellets (similar to trout pellets, which are also acceptable should *Xenopus*

The face you're looking at here belongs to a *Pseudis paradoxa*. Photo by R. T. Zappalorti.

pellets not be available). Uneaten food must be removed from the water before it rots. It is advisable to change a jugful (about 1 liter or 2 pints) of the tank water every day and to give the tank a complete cleaning and water change at three-month intervals.

Although *Xenopus laevis* is the most common clawed frog in captivity, there are at least 13 other species described from various parts of Africa. Other species in the genus, of which *X. muelleri* (9 cm, 3.8 in) from central and southern Africa is probably the most frequently available, require similar care.

FAMILY PSEUDIDAE

This family contains two genera native to South America east of the Andes.

Pseudis contains two species, including the well-known *P. paradoxus* that occurs in most of the Amazon Basin, Venezuela, the Guianas, Paraguay, and northeastern Argentina, where it inhabits lakes, rivers, and other bodies of water. Reaching 7.5 cm (3 in), its trivial name *paradoxus* arises from the paradox of its larvae being many times the length (to 25 cm, 10 in) of the adult. This phenomenon applies to all species in the family Pseudidae. The large tadpoles are prize items on the menu of native gourmets. *P.*

paradoxus is typically "frog-shaped" but has a rather small head. The eyes are large and oriented upward. The smooth skin is green to olive green or brown, with a pattern of darker blotches above, the underside being plain cream. It should be kept in a large planted aquarium with robust plants, filtered water, and a temperature in the range 24-28°C (75-82°F). Feed on a variety invertebrates, which will be snatched from the water surface. It may also be trained to take small pieces of lean meat impaled on a fine wire.

FAMILY RANIDAE

The family Ranidae contains what can be described as the typical frogs, most of which have a smooth, slippery skin and powerful hind limbs for jumping. Linnaeus, in his system of classification, placed all frogs (and toads) known at the time in the genus *Rana*, but since then this family has been revised many times and has grown to include three subfamilies, about 40 genera, and over 600 species found on every continent except Antarctica (and with very sparse representation in South America). Included in this family is the world's largest frog, the goliath frog, *Conraua goliath*, from West Africa, which grows to 40 cm (16 in) in length.

Mantella is a genus containing four species of colorful dendrobatid-like frogs all native to tropical montane forests of Madagascar. They are largely terrestrial but may climb around in low vegetation. Eggs are laid in moist situations on land and hatching larvae are washed into pools, etc., after heavy rains. They require a humid, planted terrarium with temperatures in the range 21-27°C (70-81°F), with a slight drop at night. *M. aurantiaca* from eastern Madagascar measures up to 3 cm (1.25 in) and is bright orange all over.

Conraua is a genus containing six species. It includes the giant of all frogs, *C. goliath*, which is native to Cameroon and Equatorial Guinea, where it inhabits slow-moving rivers. Growing to 40 cm (16 in) in length, this species varies in color from greenish brown to gray. It is

almost totally aquatic, feeding underwater on small vertebrates (fish, other frogs, etc.) or large invertebrates. It requires a very large aquarium with a small land area. Feed on small fish (goldfish, guppies, etc.), earthworms, and similar items. Maintain the water temperature at 25-28°C (77-82°F).

Ptychadena contains about 38 species native to sub-Saharan Africa. *P. mascariensis* is a particularly common and abundant species that often turns up in imports. In the wild it occurs from Egypt to Sierra Leone and Natal (South Africa), also on Madagascar and some Indian Ocean islands. A slim, agile frog with large eyes and a pointed snout, it grows to 7.5 cm (3 in). It varies from brown to green in color, with an attractive wide yellowish to buff dorsal stripe. It occurs in a variety of habitats from savannah to rainforest and requires an aquaterrarium with temperatures at 23-27°C (73-81°F). An increase in humidity and water depth in summer may encourage a breeding response.

Ptychadena mascareniensis **is quite abundant throughout much of Africa and grows to about 3 inches. Photo by P. Freed.**

Pyxicephalus is a genus containing just two species, including the famous *P. adspersus*, the African bullfrog. This large (the male adult at 24 cm, 9.5 in, is much larger than the female, which grows to a maximum of 12.5 cm, 5 in),

gluttonous frog has become almost as popular with the terrarium keeper as it has always been with native Africans, who find it a delicacy! Fortunately, it is a very common frog over much of Africa south of the Equator. In the more arid areas it estivates for much of the year, becoming sexually active at the onset of sudden rains, when females may lay up to 4000 eggs a piece. It is able to complete its metamorphosis in temporary waters in relatively short periods. The metamorphosed frogs are cannibalistic and will think nothing of swallowing their smaller brothers and sisters. The African bullfrog is primarily green above and its back is ornamented with a number of raised longitudinal ridges. Beneath, it is yellowish white, becoming bright yellow to orange on the throat, under the forelimbs, and in the groin. It has large canine-like projections in the lower jaw, and large specimens are capable of giving a vicious bite

In spite of its size, this species will do well in a relatively small terrarium. It should be provided with a fairly deep substrate consisting of a mixture of gravel and leaf litter, in which it will bury itself up to its eyes, ready to lunge at any passing food item. It can take a variety of large invertebrates, including earthworms, cockroaches, moths, and beetles as well as young mice. A large adult specimen is capable of swallowing a fully grown mouse, though they should not be given these too often or they will become too fat and may die prematurely. It should be provided with a fairly large water bath in which it will frequently bathe. Maintain at a temperature of about 25-28°C (77-82°F), reduced to room temperature at night. Do not keep with smaller frogs even of its own species unless you want them to disappear!

This species is unlikely to breed in the smaller terrarium though it may breed in a deep, heated pond in a greenhouse after a simulated "dry season" followed by "heavy rainfall." It is said that the males stay in the water near the spawn, defending both this and the hatchling tadpoles until they become free-swimming.

Rana is a very large genus under almost constant revision. It contains some 270 species distributed throughout the world with the exception of most of Australia and southern South America.

Rana catesbeiana is the famous American bullfrog, a large species reaching 20 cm (8 in) in length. It is usually mottled greenish to brownish, and the powerful hind limbs are usually banded in dark and

One of the largest frogs in the world is the bullfrog, *Rana catesbeiana*. It can grow as long as 8 inches. Photo by R. T. Zappalorti.

light brown. The tympanum, especially in the male, is very prominent. The male has a single vocal sac beneath the chin, with which it is able to emit its deep groaning "jug o' rum" call. Its natural range is the eastern and central United States, but in attempts to commercially harvest frog legs it has been successfully introduced to the West Coast and to other parts of the world, including parts of northern Italy. It is very aquatic in its habits and prefers large, deep but well-vegetated ponds, lakes, rivers, and marshes. It is active both by day and at night, but its call is usually emitted at dusk or during the hours of darkness.

The bullfrog must have a very large aquaterrarium with more water than land and a water depth of at least 45 cm (18 in). It should preferably be kept in a greenhouse or outdoor enclosure with a deep pool where it is much more likely to breed. Summer temperatures to 26°C (79°F) are required, with a slight reduction at night. Hibernate for two or three months at 4-5°C (39-41°F). It may be fed on a variety of large invertebrates and small vertebrates. In the wild, large specimens are known to eat small birds and snakes, though aquatic insects, crayfish, and small fish seem to be its staple diet. The tadpoles grow very large and may pass the winter in the larval stage.

Rana esculenta, the edible frog, is one species of the so-called "green frog" complex of European ranids. These are much more aquatic than their brown counterparts, and their terrestrial excursions are usually confined to sunning themselves on the banks but quickly returning to water if disturbed. Growing to about 13 cm (5 in) in length, this robust species may be predominantly green to brownish with darker markings. There may be a light dorsal stripe. The males have paired vocal sacs that protrude at the corners of the mouth during bouts of loud croaking. This species is found throughout central Europe and into Italy, but it is absent from Iberia and the Balkans.

Captive specimens require a large aquaterrarium with more water than land area. The water should be not less than 25 cm (10 in) deep. It is perhaps better suited to an outdoor enclosure with a deep pool. It will feed on a variety of invertebrates that it catches both above and below the water surface. Summer temperatures can reach 25°C (77°F) during the day, but should be reduced by a few degrees at night. An unheated terrarium should provide optimum conditions in most areas. Hibernate for about three months at 4-5°C (39-41°F). It is unlikely to breed in indoor terraria, but females may lay up to 10,000 eggs in deeper outdoor pools.

The smaller (9 cm, 3.5 in) pool frog, *R. lessonae*, and the larger (15 cm, 6 in) marsh frog, *R. ridibunda*, are similar apart

Rana esculenta, **the European edible frog, superficially resembles many of the American leopard frog species. Photo by L. Wischnath.**

from size and require similar care. All three species occur in Europe and their ranges overlap considerably in some areas. Hybridization occurs frequently, causing many taxonomic problems. It is now generally accepted that *R.*

esculenta is a sort of fertile hybrid of the other two species and contains sets of chromosomes from both.

Rana pipiens is the leopard frog so commonly mentioned in biological literature. The genus *Rana* is well represented in North America, with members of the leopard frog complex being the most abundant. *R. pipiens*, the northern leopard frog, is the common frog of the southern half of Canada and the northern half of the United States, with the exception of the western coastal areas. Reaching 8 cm (3.25 in) in length, it is a slender greenish to brownish frog with large dark spots, usually edged with gray or white. There is a light stripe along the upper jaw-line. The six to ten other leopard frog species in Canada, the United States, and Mexico are all very similar and pose enormous problems to taxonomists (a new species is still described every few years). All have similar habits, however, and may be treated similarly in captivity, allowing for differences in climates and humidity of their native range.

They are found in a variety of habitats from freshwater lakes with thick vegetation to brackish marshland and from sea level to montane meadows, mainly in or near water, where they take cover when threatened. Provide a large aquaterrarium with roughly half land and half water areas, the water to a depth of at least 15 cm (6 in). Aquatic and terrestrial plants may be used for decoration. Summer temperature to 25°C (77°F), reduced to around 15°C (59°F) at night, are acceptable. Leopard frogs should be fed on a variety of small invertebrates. *R. pipiens* breeds in captivity more readily than most other ranids and can be induced to spawn after a winter rest period by increasing the temperature and photoperiod. This species is frequently used as an experimental laboratory animal, but in many areas *Rana pipiens* and its allied species are disappearing because of land development and, perhaps, acid rain effects.

Apart from the leopard frogs, there are a number of other North American ranids that require similar husbandry.

This handsome frog is known as the Florida leopard frog, *Rana utricularia sphenocephala*. Photo by R. D. Bartlett.

These include the crawfish frog, *R. areolata* ; the green frog, *R. clamitans*; and the wood frog, *R. sylvatica*. Similar, but with a more aquatic habit, are the pig frog, *R. grylio* ; the river frog, *R. heckscheri*; and the carpenter frog, *R. virgatipes*.

Rana temporaria, the European grass frog, was probably the very first frog to get a Linnaean scientific name in 1758, but it is now just one of the 270 or so species in the same genus! *R. temporaria* is found throughout central and northern Europe as far north as the Arctic circle and east to the Ural Mountains. Like all ranid frogs, it is "typically frog-like" with a smooth, slippery skin and long, powerful hind legs that make it an excellent jumper and swimmer. The common European grass frog is a member of the "brown frog" (as opposed to the "green frog") complex. It reaches about 10 cm (4 in) in total length and is highly variable in color, ranging through shades of brown, olive, gray, yellowish, and reddish above, with darker markings. A prominent black or dark brown patch from the rear of the eye to the corner of the mouth and including the eardrum is a "trademark" of the species. The underside is an off-white with darker marbling.

This species is terrestrial for most of the year, inhabiting damp, grassy meadows, woodlands, and gardens, but it is rarely found far from permanent water. Although primarily nocturnal, it may be active during the day in secluded areas and will feed at any time if suitable prey comes into range. This species is probably best suited to an outdoor enclosure, though it may be kept in an unheated terrarium (temperatures below 20°C, 68°F) for short periods for closer observation and it can be fed on a variety of small invertebrates. It is unlikely to breed in a small aquarium, outdoor ponds being preferred; however, collected spawn can easily be reared to metamorphosis in an aquaterrarium.

FAMILY RHACOPHORIDAE

Two subfamilies with genera and species distributed from tropical Africa through Madagascar and southern Asia to Taiwan and Japan.

Philautus is a group of treefrog-like anurans inhabiting tropical rainforest. Fingers and toes are furnished with well developed adhesive disks. Most have opposing pairs of fingers that allow gripping. They require a tall, planted terrarium with high humidity and temperatures about 20-30°C (68-86°F), depending on the natural habitat of the species. *P. bimaculatus*, found from Thailand to Borneo and the Philippines, measures to 3.5 cm (1.5 in) and is brown with darker marbling and blue spots on the flanks. *P. spinosus*, from the Philippines reaches 4 cm (1.75 in). It has spiny skin that

If you look closely, you can just see the inside of this *Rana temporaria*'s mouth. Photo by L. Wischnath.

is brown, marked with lemon yellow to orange spots.

Rhacophorus is a genus containing about 60 species of arboreal frogs ranging from India to China, Japan and Southeast Asia. Most are typically "treefrog-like" in build with well developed adhesive disks on fingers and toes. Most have a very flat head with large eyes that are directed forward. The pupil is horizontal, and the tympanum usually is conspicuous. Some species have very large webbed hands

Here is a pair of Mexican burrowing toads, *Rhinophrynus dorsalis*, one of the more recently popularized frog species. Photo by R.T. Zappalorti.

and feet that, when stretched out, enable the frogs to glide up to 15 m (48 ft) between trees. Most species spawn in foliage overhanging water. About 800 eggs are laid together with a secretion that is whipped into a foam by the action of the female with her legs. The foam is impregnated with sperm from the male during amplexus. Heavy rain washes the eggs or larvae into water, where further metamorphosis takes place. Arboreal species require a tall, humid, planted terrarium with a pool of water. Temperatures will depend on where the specimen came from. *R. nigropalmatus*, found from Thailand through Malaya to Sumatra and Borneo, reaches 10 cm (4 in) in length and is light green with white spots. *R.*

Boophis opisthodon is a native of Madagascar and thrives on a large variety of tiny insects. Photo by P. Freed.

pardalis ranges from Malaya through Indonesia to the Philippines and grows to 7.5 cm (3 in). One of the "flying frogs," it is light yellowish brown with a dark cross-shaped pattern on its back.

FAMILY RHINODERMATIDAE

This family contains the single genus *Rhinoderma* with just two species of "long-nosed" frogs from southern South America. *R. darwini* from southern Chile and adjacent

Argentina inhabits the western slopes of the Andes in shady, moist woodlands close to running water. Reaching just 3 cm (1.25 in) in length, it has a sharp spine-like snout projection. The color is highly variable shades of green and brown, black beneath with white spots. The breeding habits are interesting in that clumps of eggs laid by females in moist situations on land and are "guarded" by several males for two to three weeks. On seeing the embryos move within the eggs, the males take the eggs into the mouth and pass them into the vocal sacs, where the larvae hatch and eventually metamorphose into froglets. In captivity long-nosed frogs require a moist, unheated terrarium with a mossy substrate and adequate hiding places (flat stones, hollow logs, etc.). They feed on tiny invertebrates.

FAMILY RHINOPHRYNIDAE

This family contains the single genus *Rhinophrynus* with the single species *R. dorsalis*, which ranges from southern Texas to Costa Rica. Reaching 9 cm (3.5 in) in total length, it

looks rather like a large narrowmouthed toad with an egg-shaped body and a narrow pointed head. The skin is smooth and moist. In color it is brown, with a broad orange to yellow stripe down the middle of the back. It has a large spade on each foot. It feeds principally on termites, but captive specimens will take other invertebrates. It lives in areas with loose soil where it can easily burrow. Breeding takes place in temporary pools after rainfall. It requires a large terrarium with facilities for burrowing and artificially created wet and dry seasons. Provide temperatures in the 22-28°C (72-82°F) range.

FAMILY SOOGLOSSIDAE

Contains two genera and three species native the Seychelle Islands in the Indian Ocean. All have protected status under the IUCN endangered species list and are unlikely to be available for the terrarium keeper.

The beautiful *Rhacophorus nigropalmatus* belongs to a genus containing over 60 other species. Photo by R. D. Bartlett.

Salamanders and Newts

Salamanders and newts, the caudates or tailed amphibians, belong to the order Caudata, sometimes referred to as the Urodela. Some diagnostic features of the Caudata are as follows:

1. The tail is well developed in the adult.

2. The neck is more or less distinct from the body.

3. The hind limbs (when present) are similar in length to the forelimbs and not strongly modified for jumping and/or swimming. The paired bones of the forearms are not fused.

4. The ear-drum (tympanum) is absent.

5. The skull is not completely roofed by bone.

6. The body is relatively long.

7. There is usually no voice and the larynx is poorly developed.

8. The right lung is larger than the left which is, however functional; an exception is the Plethodontidae, which is lungless.

Caudata species are much fewer in number than anurans, but with in excess of 350 species there are still too many for them all to be mentioned here. As with the Anura, however, all families and a selection of genera and species will be discussed.

FAMILY AMBYSTOMATIDAE

This rather primitive family has two genera ranging from southern Alaska and Canada through to the southern edge of the Mexican Plateau.

Ambystoma is a genus containing almost 30 species all native to North America, including Mexico. Commonly referred to as mole salamanders, many make excellent terrarium subjects. They have a robust appearance with a wide, flat head and a large mouth. The skin is smooth, well provided with glands, and usually with prominent costal grooves along the sides. Most species are very secretive and nocturnal, spending most of their time in burrows, under logs and

A rare and secretive amphibian, the ringed salamander, *Ambystoma annulatum,* is one of the most beautiful members of the mole salamander family. Photo by K. T. Nemuras.

stones, etc. They may be seen on the surface at night after rains and during the breeding season. Spawning usually takes place in still waters of ponds and lakes.

Ambystoma annulatum, the ringed salamander, reaches reaches a length of 23 cm (9.25 in). It occurs from central Missouri to western Arkansas and eastern Oklahoma. It has a relatively small head and a slender body that is deep brown to black above, marked with narrow cream to yellow bands along the body and tail. The lower sides are light gray, and the underside is slate colored with lighter spots. It inhabits damp forested areas or clearings in hilly areas, particularly in the region of the Ouachita and Ozark Mountains. It breeds in ponds or temporary pools after autumn rains. In captivity it requires an unheated terrarium with good ventilation and prepared in the woodland style. Feed on a variety of small invertebrates.

Ambystoma laterale, the blue-spotted salamander, measures up to 12.5 cm (5 in). It is a relatively slender salamander with a narrow snout and short limbs. It is blackish blue above with light blue spots and blotches. The underside is grayish blue with darker blotching. It is found throughout the Great Lakes region east to the Atlantic coast of North America. Its main habitat is near water in deciduous forests, where it burrows under ground debris. Mating occurs in ponds during March and April. The female lays several batches of 10-15 eggs that are attached to aquatic vegetation or debris. Larvae hatch in about 30 days and metamorphose to terrestrial forms in four to six months. In captivity it should be provided with a small aquaterrarium containing leaf litter. The humidity should be kept high. Summer temperatures of 15-20°C (59-68°F) are adequate. During the winter, keep at just above freezing (3-4°C, 38-39°F) for two to three months for simulated hibernation. It should be fed on a selection of small invertebrates.

Ambystoma jeffersonianum, Jefferson's salamander, grows to a length of 20 cm (8 in). It is a rather plain looking species but is a good terrarium subject. It is relatively long and slender, with a ground color of dark brown to brownish gray above; occasionally there are bluish flecks on the limbs and lower flanks. It is found in deciduous forests in the northeastern United States, where it usually burrows under surface debris near areas of permanent water. In captivity it requires a cool (15-20°C, 59-68°F) aquaterrarium. It will feed on a

Shown here is a gorgeous blue-spotted salamander, *Ambystoma laterale*. Photo by R. T. Zappalorti.

variety of small vertebrates. This species is known to hybridize with *A. laterale*, producing all-female offspring.

Ambystoma maculatum, the spotted salamander, measures up to 25 cm (10 in) and is one of the larger and more interesting species in the family, this salamander has well developed limbs. Being spectacular in color and relatively easy to keep, it has become a very popular pet species. The ground color is blue-gray and there are two rows of large yellow or orange spots starting on top of the head and extending to the tail tip. The underside is usually a plain slate color. In the wild, this species occurs throughout eastern North America from Nova Scotia and the Great Lakes almost to the Gulf Coast. It is found mainly in areas of deciduous woodland, rarely far from permanent water. It is an adept burrower and spends most of its time below the surface, emerging at night or after heavy rains. It may breed at various times of the year in different parts of its range. Northern specimens, for example, will breed from March to April, while southern examples breed from December to February. Clumps of about 100 eggs are laid attached to submerged debris in breeding ponds. The larvae hatch in four to eight weeks, full metamorphosis occurring 8-16 weeks later. Captive specimens require a large woodland terrarium and will require access to water if breeding is contemplated. The humidity should be kept high. Supplementary heating should not be required; in fact, try to keep the temperature not higher than 25°C (77°F). Feed on various small invertebrates.

Ambystoma opacum, the marbled salamander, at a length of just 12 cm (5 in) is one of the smaller members of the genus. However, it is robustly built with well-developed limbs. This species is black with steel-gray marbling above, while the underside is plain black. It occurs in a variety of woodland sites in the eastern United States, from the Great Lakes to the Gulf States,

One of the hardiest, most attractive amphibians is the spotted salamander, *Ambystoma maculatum*. Photo by R. T. Zappalorti.

transform into fully terrestrial forms in four to six months. In captivity, it requires a medium-sized, humid terrarium with summer temperature to 25°C (77°F). Reduce the temperature for a period of simulated hibernation in the winter.

Ambystoma tigrinum, the tiger salamander, attains a maximum length of 22 cm (8.5 in) and is one of the world's largest land-dwelling salamander species. (Neotenic specimens have attained 33 cm, 12.9 in.) It is a broad-headed and robust species that quickly becomes accustomed to captivity and makes a fine pet. There are several subspecies displaying a huge variation in color and pattern. The ground color may be greenish, grayish, or brown with yellow to white spots, stripes, or marbling. It is very widespread across the USA from coast to coast and extends into Mexico. It occurs in varied habitats from damp woodland to fairly dry savannah. A secretive burrowing species, wild tiger salamanders are rarely seen during the daytime unless the collector is particularly looking for them in deep leaf litter, under and in

but does not occur on the Florida peninsula. This is the only member of the genus that does not spawn in water. Mating occurs on land and the eggs are laid in damp depressions that later fill with rainwater, the female curling around and protecting the eggs from desiccation until it rains. After hatching, the larvae decaying logs, etc. Courtship and mating take place in temporary pools, lakes, or streams in springtime. The eggs are laid in masses attached to aquatic vegetation. The larvae transform in five to six months. Western populations may be neotenic and remain in the water, eventually reproducing in larval form. Captive specimens require a large aquaterrarium or an aquarium for neotenic specimens. A temperature range of 15-20°C (59-68°F) will suit them fine. Feed on a variety of invertebrates. Hibernate in winter.

FAMILY AMPHIUMIDAE

This family contains a single genus with only three species, making it the smallest salamander family. All three are native to southeastern USA and are totally aquatic burrowers internal gills opening just in front of the extremely reduced forelimbs.

Amphiuma means, the two-toed amphiuma, reaches a total length of 100 cm (39 in) and is probably the best known of the three amphiumas. It is a robust, eel-like animal with four tiny limbs, each with only two toes. There are no external gills, and the tiny eyes are lidless. In color it is uniformly dark gray to brown above with a lighter gray underside. It is found in mainly acidic, vegetated, muddy waters including swamps, bayous, and ditches in the southeastern coastal plain of the United States from southeastern Virginia to Mississippi and adjacent Louisiana. It is largely nocturnal, hiding during the day in submerged burrows. In moist weather conditions it can migrate overland. It feeds mainly on crayfish, but will take frogs, other salamanders, fishes, and even small water snakes. In captivity it will do well in a large, well-aerated aquarium with a gravel substrate and larger rocks securely arranged to create hiding caves. Aquatic plants will soon be uprooted by the animals, so only floating plants should be used. The temperature of water should be maintained at about 24°C (75°F), reduced to 18°C (65°F) in winter for a couple of months. The water must be chlorine-free and unpolluted.

The unusual three-toed amphiuma, *Amphiuma tridactylum*, breeds in the spring. Photo by P. Freed.

Feed on tadpoles, small fishes, and pieces of lean meat or heart, etc., if you cannot get living crayfish.

Amphiumas breed in the spring and fertilization is internal. The female seeks out a sheltered depression in the shallows where she lays about 200 eggs and remains coiled about them until they hatch (usually about 5 months). The larvae are about 5 cm (2 in) long and have external gills like most salamander larvae but they lose these as they mature, just retaining the adult pair of gill slits. The other two species in the genus are *A. pholeter*, the one-toed and *A. tridactylum*, the three-toed amphiuma, which have similar habits and require similar husbandry.

FAMILY CRYPTOBRANCHIDAE

Contains two genera and only three species.

Andrias contains two closely related species, *A. davidianus* from China and *A. japonicus* from Japan, which are the world's largest salamanders. These aquatic giants reach a maximum length of 1.8 and 1.4 m (6 ft and 4ft 8 in) respectively. Living in clear mountain streams (occasionally in mountain lakes), these giant salamanders are strictly protected as endangered species (at least in theory, though the Chinese species often appears in food markets) and, as such, are unlikely to fall into the hands of the pet keeper, though they may still be seen in the large aquaria at some zoos. Massive in build, with a flap of loose skin (presumably to increase area of respiration) along the flanks, *Andrias* has no external gills or gill slits. Lungs are present, but most respiration takes place through the skin. The color is dark brownish to steel gray. Breeding takes place in the summer, when the male excavates a chamber in the mud into which he induces the female to lay her 400-500 eggs that are joined together with mucus to form a chain. The male fertilizes the eggs and then guards them until they hatch into free-swimming larvae. In captivity they require a deep aquarium with crystal clear, unpolluted water and temperatures not greater than 18°C (65°F), preferably less.

Cryptobranchus is a monotypic genus containing the species *C. alleganiensis*, the hellbender. Growing to a length of 75 cm (30 in), this American relation of the Asian giant salamanders is a large, totally aquatic amphibian with a flattened head and body; a loose flap of skin runs along the lower flanks. It has moderately large limbs with four fingers and five toes. There are no external feathery gills, but there is a single pair of gill openings just behind the head. It is grayish brown with darker mottling above, while the underside is lighter and uniform. The male is somewhat smaller than the female. Found in the central and eastern United States, the hellbender prefers fast-flowing rivers and streams, especially those with rocky bottoms. It usually hides under rocks or in cavities during the day, coming out at night to hunt for food. It feeds on a variety of invertebrates and vertebrates and in captivity will take strips of raw meat or fish. It should be kept only in very large, well-aerated aquaria with a stony substrate and caves for seclusion. Supplementary heating is unnecessary, and the temperature should be reduced

In recent years, the commercial popularity of the hellbender, *Cryptobranchus alleganiensis*, has actually grown quite a bit. Photo by R. T. Zappalorti.

in the winter. The animals breed in the late summer to fall, the male excavating a nest cavity beneath large flat rocks or submerged logs. The female lays 200-500 eggs in strings that are sprayed with milt by the male then pushed together into a tangled mass in the nest cavity. The male guards the nest until the approximately 2.5 cm (1 in) larvae hatch in two to three months.

FAMILY DICAMPTODONTIDAE

This family, only recently separated from Ambystomatidae and not accepted by all workers, is divided into two subfamilies.

Subfamily Dicamptodontinae

Dicamptodon, the only genus in the subfamily, has two or three species. *D. ensatus*, the Pacific giant salamander a robust, smooth-skinned species which reaches a length of 30 cm (12 in). The ground color above is brownish to purplish with a darker mottling. The underside is pale brown to off-white. It occurs in western coastal North America from British Columbia to northern California. There is an isolated population in the Rockies in Idaho and western Montana that is believed by some to be a separate species, *D. aterrimus*. These salamanders inhabit the cool, humid forests surrounding rivers and their tributaries. Some populations are neotenous and spend their whole lives as aquatic larvae, breeding in that condition. Terrestrial adults mate in the spring in river headwaters. In captivity, terrestrial adults require a large aquaterrarium with well-aerated water. They may be fed on large invertebrates. The closely related *D. copei* (Cope's giant salamander) from the Olympic Peninsula in Washington is similar to the larva of *D. ensatus* but appears to never transform to a terrestrial stage in the wild though, as with the axolotl, this may be artificially accomplished in the laboratory.

Subfamily Rhyacotritoninae

Contains only a single genus.

Rhyacotriton contains the single species *R. olympicus*, the Olympic salamander, which

Although most salamanders have no voice, the Pacific giant salamander, *Dicamptodon ensatus*, will shriek when angered. Photo by K. Lucas, Steinhart Aquarium.

grows to a total length of 11 cm (4.5 in). It is a small, plainly colored salamander that is quite agile but is not named after its athletic abilities, but rather after the Olympic Mountains in Washington where it was first discovered. Its eyes are very prominent and set high on its head. It occurs in coastal regions of the Pacific Northwest south to California and inhabits areas near or in fast-moving streams, often in the splash zone among mossy boulders. It requires an aquaterrarium with pure, turbulent water splashing over pebbles. Being a somewhat "difficult" captive, this species is not recommended for the beginner.

FAMILY PLETHODONTIDAE

This is the largest salamander family, containing 2 subfamilies, 27 genera, and over 220 species. Many are fraught with taxonomic problems and much remains to be learned about their biology. Commonly known as "lungless salamanders" (they respire through the sensitive moist skin), the plethodontids are primarily found in the New World from southern Alaska and Nova Scotia through Mexico and Central America to Brazil and Bolivia. Two isolated species are found in southern Europe. Many new species have been described in recent years, most of these being from Mexico and Central America, and there is no reason to assume that there are still more species waiting to be discovered and named.

Subfamily Desmognathinae

Contains three genera, all native to southeastern Canada and the eastern United States.

Desmognathus is a genus containing about a dozen species of generally robust semi-aquatic salamanders native to southeastern Canada and the eastern United States, west to eastern Oklahoma and Texas. They have an unusual skull structure in which the upper jaw is movable upward, very unusual in amphibians. All species in the genus require a cool aquaterrarium, though some species are more aquatic than others. With southern species maintain a slightly

higher summer temperatures (20-22°C, 68-72°F) than northern ones (18-20°, 65C). In winter the northern species should be hibernated for two to four months, while southern species can be kept four to six weeks at reduced temperatures (10-12°C, 50-54°F). Feed on a variety of small invertebrates.

Desmognathus auriculatus, the southern dusky salamander, is found on the coastal plain, ranging from southeastern Virginia to central Florida and eastern Texas. Reaching 15 cm (6 in), it has a dark brown to black body and a row of whitish or reddish spots along the flanks; the underside is brown, speckled with white. *D. fuscus,* the dusky salamander (length to 15 cm, 6 in) occurs over much of the eastern United States. Its color is variable, tan to dark brown above, plain or mottled, sometimes with a vertebral stripe. Two dwarf species from the southern Appalachian Mountains, *D. aeneus,* the seepage salamander, and *D. wrighti,* . the pigmy salamander, seldom exceed 5.5 cm (2.1 in) in length and are almost completely

**A mountain dusky salamander,
Desmognathus ochrophaeus.
Photo by R. T. Zappalorti.**

terrestrial, lacking an aquatic
larval stage, the young
maturing within the egg.

Subfamily Plethodontinae

Contains 24 genera. Several
genera have very broad
distributions in the United

States, with species common in
moist habitats anywhere near
higher elevations in the east. In
the tropics there are many
genera (some recently
discovered or distinguished)
associated with bromeliads.
This subfamily comprises over
half of all described
salamanders living today, and
there are indications that many
more species are still to be
discovered.

Aneides has five species native to the western and eastern United States. *A. aeneus*, the green salamander, reaches 12 cm (5 in) and is an attractive species marbled in black and glossy green to yellow-green along the back damp, hilly, forested areas, hiding under logs or in rock crevices during the day and emerging at night to hunt small prey. It requires a cool, heavily planted woodland terrarium and a winter hibernation period. Like most lungless

from the head to the tail tip. The limbs are usually reddish brown, and the flanks and underside are mottled brownish. There are 14-15 costal grooves; the rear part of the head appears to be swollen. It occurs in the Appalachian Mountains from southwestern Pennsylvania to central Alabama. Usually it is found in

The black salamander, *Aneides flavipunctatus*, has a very small range, only being found in northern California. Photo by K. Lucas.

salamanders, it breeds on land. The eggs are laid in a secluded hollow and guarded by the female until they hatch. Full

The California slender salamander, *Batrachoseps attenuatus,* is a commonly seen animal, particularly after heavy rains. Photo by K. Lucas, Steinhart Aquarium.

metamorphosis occurs in the egg, and the hatchlings are miniature versions of adults.

Aneides lugubris, the arboreal salamander from the coastal ranges of California and the Baja peninsula, is a slender species with a relatively large head and a somewhat prehensile tail. The upper parts are gray-brown to chocolate with small yellow or cream spots; the underside is creamy white. It is an adept climber and often hides in hollow limbs far from the ground, to which it frequently descends. Its breeding habits are similar to those of the green salamander. It requires a tall, planted terrarium with several hollow logs and slabs of bark. Humidity should be high and the temperature to 25°C (77°F) in summer (cooler at night) and 18°C (65°F) in winter. Feed on small invertebrates.

Batrachoseps is a genus containing eight species, the slender salamanders from the western part of North America. *B. attenuatus*, the California slender salamander, is probably the best known, is abundant in its range, and frequently is seen abroad after rainfall. Reaching 15 cm (6 in), it occurs from extreme southwestern Oregon south along the coastal ranges to southwestern California, where it inhabits montane forest, hiding during the day in moist ground litter or in rotting limbs. Like all members of the genus, it has a slender, elongated body and tail. It is brown to black with a very broad yellow, light brown, or reddish vertebral band, often marked with a row of dark chevrons. Beneath, it is black marked with white spots. It breeds on land and there is no aquatic larval stage. It requires a moist woodland terrarium with summer temperatures to 25°C (77°F), reduced at night and in winter.

Bolitoglossa is a genus containing over 66 species native to Central and South America, where they may be found in a great range of biotopes. They are mostly fairly thickset salamanders with short limbs and webbed fingers and toes. Housing and temperatures will depend on their natural habitats, but beware of overheating. *B. adspersa*, reaching 10 cm (4 in), is from Colombia and is dark brown in color with a light brown pattern. It inhabits high altitudes and should be kept at temperatures not exceeding 22°C (72°F). *B. altamazonica*, from the lower slopes of the Andes from Colombia to Bolivia and the upper Amazon valley in Brazil, measures up to 9 cm (3.5 in). It is dark gray to brown with whitish blotches along the flanks and limbs. It requires a rainforest terrarium with temperatures to 26°C (79°F).

Ensatina is a monotypic genus containing the species *E. eschscholtzii*, the ensatina, which occurs from southern British Columbia south along the Pacific ranges to Baja California, living in a variety of habitats. It grows to 15 cm (6 in). Its tail is constricted at its base, a character seldom seen in salamanders in the United States. There is great variation in color and pattern among the seven subspecies ranging, from uniformly brown to reddish brown, dark brown or black, with yellow, cream, or orange spots or mottling. The underside is usually plain whitish. The most attractive subspecies is probably *E. e.*

platensis, from the Sierra Nevadas, which is light brown with large orange spots. It requires a relatively moist woodland terrarium with a temperature not greater than 22°C (72°F). Breeding is wholly terrestrial.

Hydromantes is a genus containing five species native to the western United States and central southern Europe. *H. italicus*, the Italian cave salamander, is one of only two European plethodontid

When keeping certain members of the genus *Bolitoglossa*, you have to be very careful not to overheat them. Photo of *Bolitoglossa altamazonica* by R. T. Zappalorti.

salamanders (the other being *H. geneii*, the Sardinian cave salamander). Measuring up to 12.5 cm (5 in), it is reddish brown in color with a marbling of yellowish to pinkish. The underside is usually dark with whitish marbling. It occurs in extreme southeastern France across northern Italy and extending to central Italy on the eastern half of the peninsula. It lives in moist, rocky situations, under stones, logs, etc., and is nocturnal, retreating deep into crevices during longer periods of dry weather. In captivity it requires a moist terrarium provided with rocks and ferns. Maintain the summer daytime temperature at 25°C (77°F), reduced to 15°C (59°F) at night, with a winter temperature range of 10-20°C (50-68°F). Feed on a variety of small vertebrates. Breeding habits similar to *Aneides aeneus*.

Plethodon is a genus containing about 27 species native to North America. *P. cinereus*, the redback salamander, is one of the best known in the genus. It is found in many parts of the northeastern quarter of the USA and adjacent southeastern

Canada, including Newfoundland. Growing to 12.5 cm (5 in), it has a long and slender appearance. There are two color phases, the most attractive being the true "red-backed," which has a wide, usually red, vertebral band extending from the head to the tip of the tail. The band may occasionally be yellow, pink, orange, or gray. The "lead-backed" is light gray to almost black without the vertebral stripe. The underside is mottled in black and white. It inhabits most kinds of woodland within its range, hiding and foraging under rocks or ground litter and usually only surfacing after heavy rainfall. Eggs are laid in midsummer in a cluster suspended from the roof of a cavity below a stone or log. The female guards these until they hatch about eight weeks later. In captivity they require an unheated, moist, woodland terrarium planted with moss and ferns and with adequate hiding places (flat stones, bark, etc.). Do not allow the temperature to exceed 20°C (68°F) in summer. Allow to hibernate in winter.

Plethodon glutinosus, the

The red-backed salamander, *Plethodon cinereus*, is a highly abundant and completely terrestrial amphibian. Photo by G. Dingerkus.

slimy salamander, is a relatively long (20 cm, 8 in), slender species with a round body and a flattened head. It is mainly black with cream or white spots concentrated along the flanks. The underside is slate blue, often mottled with white. It occurs in the eastern USA and into southeastern Canada, where it is found in a range of habitats from near sea level to 1600 meters (5200 ft). It hides under rocks and fallen timber, emerging at night to forage. Handle with care as its skin secretes a sticky substance that is difficult to remove! The female lays 10-35 eggs in summer in a secluded cavity below ground litter. She guards them until they hatch about eight weeks later. It requires a medium sized, cool terrarium with a gravel and leaf-litter substrate and a few flat stones and plants. Provide a period of simulated hibernation in the winter. Recent work with molecular biology has broken the slimy salamander into 13 full species that are largely identical in superficial appearance and best separated by geography. See one of the newer North American field guides for details.

Pseudotriton contains three species native to the eastern United States. *P. ruber*, the red salamander, is one of the most colorful North American salamanders and much prized in the terrarium. It reaches a maximum length of about 17.5 cm (7 in). There are four subspecies ranging from bright orange-red to purplish above, with numerous small black spots. The underside is pinkish and may be spotted with black. It occurs in the eastern USA except for the southeastern coastal plain and most of Florida. Found in very moist habitats, particularly around springs and seepages to altitudes of 1500 meters (4875 ft), it is nocturnal, hiding under cover during the day. It requires a large terrarium with a high humidity. A gravel substrate and mossy rocks will provide the furnishings. Try to provide an artificial drip seepage. Unlike most plethodontid salamanders (but like many other species found in the eastern United States),

the eggs are laid in shallow water and hatch into larvae that metamorphose in 2-2.5 years.

FAMILY PROTEIDAE

This family contains two genera, one native to eastern North America, the other to Yugoslavia.

Necturus is a genus with five species of totally aquatic salamanders found in the eastern United States. The largest and best known of these is *N. maculosus*, the mudpuppy, which reaches a maximum length of 45 cm (18 in). The mudpuppies and waterdogs derived their English name from the erroneous belief that they could bark, but, in fact, their vocal talents are confined to a weakish squeak. The mudpuppy is a robust aquatic species with four fingers and four toes and a pair of dark red feathery gills. It is gray-brown to dark gray above with dark-edged bluish blotches, while the underside is usually gray with darker markings. Occurring in central and eastern North America, it may be found in streams, rivers, and lakes. In captivity

The attractive red salamander, *Pseudotriton ruber*, is really not all that difficult to maintain in captivity. Photo by R. T. Zappalorti.

mudpuppies require a large aquarium with filtered and aerated water to a depth of at least 30 cm (12 in). The substrate may be medium grade gravel, decorated with larger stones and tree roots. Feed mudpuppies on small fish, freshwater shrimp, water snails, and other aquatic animals. Breeding occurs in late spring. The female lays up to 200 eggs attached beneath rocks, roots, or other debris. These hatch into 2 cm (0.8 in) larvae that take up to five years to mature. Other species in the genus are generally much smaller; *N. alabamensis*, the Alabama waterdog, for example, reaches a maximum length of 20 cm (8 in). Habits and care are similar for all species, but the waterdogs will, of course, require smaller accommodations.

Proteus is a monotypic genus containing the species *P. anguinus*, the olm, which is a rarely seen, secretive species from subterranean streams and lakes in limestone caves in the eastern Adriatic seaboard of Yugoslavia. There is also an isolated population in northeastern Italy. Reaching a total length of 30 cm (12 in), the olm is a large aquatic salamander that is uniformly pinkish white in color with large, feathery, salmon-pink gills. The limbs are poorly developed, with three fingers and two toes. The eyes are very small and the snout is extended like that of a pike. This species has been successfully kept and bred in captivity through several successive generations. It requires a cooled (6-12°C, 43-54°F), unlighted aquarium (a light may be used for occasional observation purposes) with a sandy bottom and several limestone rocks. Feed frequently but sparingly on small aquatic invertebrates (waterfleas, tubifex worms, mosquito larvae, etc.) or very small earthworms. The water should be crystal clear, filtered, and be maintained at a pH of not less than 7.6. Females may produce yolk-rich eggs or living larvae. Larvae grow to sexually mature adults over several years.

FAMILY SALAMANDRIDAE

This group, commonly called the family of typical salamanders and newts, includes 14 genera and some 53 species occurring mostly in Eurasia and North Africa, with only two genera, *Notophthalmus* and *Taricha* occur in the New World.

Chioglossa is a monotypic genus containing the species *C. lusitanica*, the golden-striped salamander. With a total adult length of 15 cm (6 in), this species has an extremely slender appearance and the eyes are set high on the head. Along the flanks there are distinct costal grooves. It is brownish above, with two broad golden to copper-colored stripes extending along either side of the back and joining to form a single stripe along the tail. Confined to the northern half of Portugal and adjacent northwestern Spain, this species is mainly nocturnal,

The Alabama waterdog, *Necturus alabamensis*, is a voracious eater, taking everything from snails and worms to crayfish. Photo by R. D. Bartlett.

hiding under stones and ground litter during the day. It occurs only in moist mountainous areas and, when disturbed, it produces a surprisingly lizard-like turn of speed. Captive specimens require a cool (not greater than 20°C, 68°F) aquaterrarium planted with mosses and ferns. Reduce the temperature in winter (Dec., Jan.) for simulated hibernation. Feed on small invertebrates including flies, which this species is adept at catching with its long, sticky tongue.

Cynops is a genus containing seven species native to southern and eastern China and Japan. The best known species in the genus is probably *C. pyrrhogaster*, the Japanese red-bellied newt, which grows to a length of 10 cm (4 in). It is dark chocolate brown above and brilliant, fiery red below. In the nuptial season, the male's tail becomes bluish or purplish. Almost totally aquatic, it inhabits vegetated ponds only on the Japanese islands of Honshu, Shikoku, and Kyushu. A closely related species (*C. ensicauda*) occurs on the Ryukyu Islands south of Japan. In captivity the Japanese red-belly requires an aquarium with aerated and filtered water to a depth of 20 cm (8 in) and land areas such as mossy rocks or tree roots breaking the surface. Summer temperatures should be maintained around 25°C (77°F), but can be reduced to between 5 and 10°C (41-50°F) for a couple of months of simulated hibernation. Feed on small aquatic invertebrates. Breeding occurs in the springtime, when courtship and mating take place in water. The eggs are laid on the leaves of aquatic plants.

Euproctus is a genus containing just three species, one of which is *E. montanus*, the Corsican brook salamander. With a total adult length of 12 cm (4 in), it is the smallest of the three species of European brook salamanders, the other two being *E. asper* (Pyrenean) and *E. platycephalus* (Sardinian). This species is brown to olive above, occasionally with greenish or yellowish markings forming a vertebral line. Below, it is grayish white to brown, often with white flecks. It occurs in or near mountain streams on the French Mediterranean island of Corsica. During the hotter, dryer periods of the year it estivates deep in some crevice. It requires an unheated aquarium with shallow, filtered, aerated water and a few landing places. Reduce the temperature in winter for a couple of months for simulated hibernation. Feed on small invertebrates.

A beautiful example of the Japanese red-bellied newt, *Cynops pyrrhogaster*. Photo by B. Kahl.

Notophthalmus contains three species native to eastern North America. The best known is *N. viridescens*, the red-spotted newt, which grows to a total adult length of 12 cm (5 in). This newt is noted for the remarkable differences in appearance between the aquatic adults and the juvenile terrestrial form. Adults are smooth-skinned and yellowish brown to olive-brown above with dark-bordered red spots along each side of the body, sometimes almost forming a line. The underside is yellowish and there are small dark spots all over the body. The terrestrial juveniles, known as red efts, were once thought to be an entirely separate species. These have a rough skin texture and are bright reddish brown to orange all over, with spots of lighter red along the flanks. They are found in eastern North America from southern Canada and the Great Lakes region to Florida and eastern Texas. Adults are mainly aquatic, living in shallow vegetated waters. In captivity they require a large aquaterrarium that will support both terrestrial and aquatic

stages. The temperature should preferably not exceed 22°C (72°F) in summer and should be reduced to around 5°C (41°F) in winter for hibernation. Courtship occurs in water. Some 200-400 eggs are laid singly, attached to aquatic vegetation. Gilled larvae hatch in three to eight weeks and eventually metamorphose into the red efts, which spend one or more years on land before returning to the water as mature adults.

Pleurodeles is a genus containing two species native to southwestern Europe and North Africa. *P. waltl*, the sharp-ribbed newt, is Europe's largest salamander, though relatively few specimens actually reach the maximum recorded length of 30 cm (12 in). It is heavily built with a broad, flattened head; the skin is rough with a row of yellow or orange warty tubercles along the flanks, through which the sharp tips of the ribs may protrude. The upper side is olive to grayish yellow with dark brown patches; older specimens are often darker in color. Beneath, the color is yellow to off-white or gray,

The popular red-spotted newt, *Notophthalmus viridescens viridescens,* will attain an adult length of just under half a foot. Photo by K. T. Nemuras.

usually with darker blotches. It is native to the southwestern two-thirds of the Iberian peninsula and Morocco, where it inhabits water courses, lakes, ditches, and irrigation systems and is mainly aquatic unless water sources dry up, in which case it estivates until conditions again become favorable. In captivity it requires a planted aquarium with facilities to land (floating platform or rock breaking surface). Feed on larger invertebrates such as

Left: An attractive pair of California newts, *Taricha torosa*. Photo by I. Francais.

Opposite: When threatened, *Taricha torosa* will bend back in defense and reveal a bright yellow belly. Photo by H. Hansen.

submersed debris.

Taricha is a genus containing three species that replace *Notophthalmus* on the western side of North America. *T. torosa*, the California newt, and its close relatives *T. granulosa* (rough-skinned newt) and *T. rivularis* (red-bellied newt) are very similar in general appearance. The California newt is a robust species reaching 18 cm (7 in) in length. Its skin is granular and tan to reddish brown above, orange to yellow below. During the breeding season the male's skin becomes smooth and his tail becomes compressed. If alarmed or attacked by predators, this species arches its body to expose the red underside. Found in coastal California and the California Sierras, where it inhabits evergreen and oak forests near permanent water, it is

earthworms, freshwater shrimp, crickets, etc. May also take small strips of lean meat. Maintain at 25°C (77°F) in summer and reduce to around 8°C (46°F) for a winter rest period. Courtship occurs in the water. The male deposits a spermatophore that is taken up by the female. Up to 1000 eggs are laid in clumps on water plants or other

terrestrial except for in the breeding season. Captive specimens should be provided with a large aquaterrarium with a planted land area. Keep at 22°C (72°F) during the summer, reduced to around 10°C (50°F) for a couple of months in winter. Feed on a variety of small invertebrates. These newts breed in water from December to May and lay their eggs on aquatic plants. Larvae may metamorphose during the first season or in the following spring.

Salamandra is a genus containing two species native to Eurasia and North Africa. *S. salamandra*, the fire salamander, is *the* salamander of folklore. It is a handsome animal endowed with a livery of bright yellow or orange on a glossy black background. The yellow markings may be arranged in spots, blotches, or stripes, depending on geographical variation. There are 11 subspecies occurring in western, central, and southern Europe, northwestern Africa, and parts of southwestern Asia. It usually inhabits heavily forested areas in hilly or mountainous country, though there are some lowland populations in suitable areas. It lives in damp conditions rarely far from water and hides under ground litter during the day, coming out at night to hunt for food. In captivity it should be provided with a large unheated aquaterrarium with moving aerated water. It should be provided with adequate refuges such as flat stones, hollow branches, etc. Feed on a variety of invertebrates. Hibernate in winter at lower temperatures. Courtship and mating occur on land, and the female deposits developed larvae into suitable waters.

Triturus contains 12 species of typical European newts (the alpine newt, *T. alpestris*, has been described in some detail earlier) that occur in Eurasia.

Although the pattern and coloration of this fire salamander, *Salamandra salamandra*, are stunning, it is an unusual variant and not likely encountered. Photo by J. Coborn.

One of the best known is *T. cristatus*, the great-crested or warty newt, which reaches a total length of 17.5 cm (7 in). It occurs in western, central, and eastern Europe, extending into Asia. It has a black, warty skin with fine white spots along the flanks. The underside is bright yellow to orange with black spots. During the aquatic

breeding season the male takes on a special courtship dress that includes a high, spiky crest along the spine and running into the flattened tail, which also sports a bluish white flash. After breeding, it reverts to resemble the female. It usually occurs near static water, particularly in alkaline soil areas. In some parts of its range it may remain aquatic throughout the year, but in others it leaves the water after breeding and becomes nocturnal and secretive. In captivity it requires an unheated aquaterrarium. Allow it to hibernate in the winter.

Triturus marmoratus, the marbled newt, is an attractive species, being marbled with green, brown, and black. There is a yellow vertebral stripe, and the underside is gray to whitish with darker mottling. During the breeding season the male develops a prominent untoothed dorsal crest. Its natural range is southwestern France and the Iberian peninsula, where it replaces *T. cristatus*. Where the ranges of the two species overlap, hybrids of great beauty may occur. *T. marmoratus* spends most of the year on land, often in relatively dry situations. In captivity it should have a large aquaterrarium maintained at 20-25°C (68-77°F), with a reduction to around 10°C (50°F) for simulated hibernation. Feed on a variety of small invertebrates. The marbled newt breeds in the water in the earlier part of the year.

Triturus vittatus, the banded newt, grows to a length of 15 cm (6 in). In its breeding dress the male banded newt must be the most spectacular of all newts, especially the subspecies *T. v. ophryticus*. The ground color is reddish brown, covered with small dark spots. A broad, black-bordered, silvery white stripe extends along the flanks between the limbs. The underside is yellow to orange. The crest of the breeding male is deeply serrated and as much as twice the depth of the body, while the broad, flattened tail is also crested on both edges and is marked with blue and green blotches. This species occurs in Asia Minor and adjacent Russian states through southeastern Turkey to northern Iraq, Syria, Lebanon, and Israel, where it usually inhabits moist areas above 1000 meters (3250 ft). It requires a medium aquaterrarium with the temperature to 25°C (77°F) in summer, reduced in winter for hibernation. Feed on a variety of small invertebrates. Breeding habits are similar to those of *T. cristatus*.

Triturus vulgaris is the common European or smooth newt, which reaches a length of 10 cm (4 in). Outside the breeding season, this little newt is fairly drab in appearance; in full breeding dress, however, the male takes on a breath-taking beauty. He develops a high, continuous wavy crest, large dark blotches develop on the body, a bluish flash develops along the lower margin of the tail, and the orange color of the belly intensifies. The female is usually olive brown with a less intense belly color and smaller black spots. As its name implies, this is an abundant species in much of Europe and into Asia, though it is absent from Iberia, being replaced there by *T. boscai*. Mainly terrestrial, it spends the days under ground litter in damp situations rarely far from permanent water. Provide a medium-sized aquaterrarium with adequate hiding places on land. It breeds in spring after entering water.

FAMILY SIRENIDAE

This family contains two genera and three species, all native to North America. Known as sirens, these remarkable aquatic, gilled amphibians have no hind limbs, tiny forelimbs, and an eel-like body.

Pseudobranchus is a monotypic genus containing the species *P. striatus*, the dwarf siren, which reaches a length of 25 cm (10 in). It is brown to light gray above, with a lighter stripe along the back and another along each flank. It has external gills and a single gill slit. The forefeet have three toes. It is native to the coastal plain of South Carolina, Georgia, and peninsular Florida, where it inhabits thickly vegetated shallow waters including ditches, ponds, and swamps. It breeds in spring, when eggs are laid singly on water plants. In captivity it requires similar care to *S. lacertina*.

Siren is a genus containing two species. *S. lacertina*, the greater siren, is the largest species in the family, reaching

A pair of common newts, *Triturus vulgaris*, shown in the aquarium. Photo by L. Wischnath.

a total adult length of 100 cm (39 in). It has a stout, eel-like, body that is gray to olive above, occasionally with darker spots. The flanks are lighter in color with many faint yellowish blotches. It has external gills and three pairs of gill slits. The forefeet have four toes. The vertically flattened tail is rounded at the tip. The greater siren is native to the coastal plain of the southeastern United Stated from the District of Columbia to Florida and Alabama, where it occurs in shallow, muddy, highly vegetated waters. In captivity it requires a large aquarium with a deep substrate (fine gravel or sand) and a water depth of about 35 cm (14 in). Keep the water at 25°C (77°F), reduced to 18°C (65°F) in winter. Feed on small fish, snails, insect larvae, and aquatic plants.

CAECILIANS

The caecilians are the least known group of amphibians. Members of the order Gymnophiona, sometimes referred to as Apoda, most of them are very secretive and are usually burrowing, but some are aquatic. Inhabiting the tropical forests, they are more or less circumtropical in distribution, occurring in Central and South America, Africa, and Asia. Caecilians superficially resemble large earthworms, having a cylindrical body with numerous transverse rings. Legs and tail are absent. Some diagnostic features of the Gymnophiona are as follows:

1. The tail is absent or rudimentary in the adult.

2. There is no distinct neck, the head being apparently continuous with the body, which bears numerous transverse rings.

3. There are no limbs or girdles.

4. The eyes are reduced and usually covered by skin and/or bone.

5. There is a sensory tentacle protruding through an aperture near the eye.

6. The ear-drum (tympanum) is absent.

7. The skull is almost completely roofed by bone.

8. The body is relatively elongate and worm-like.

9. There is no voice (the larynx is absent).

10. Only the right lung is typically functional, the left rudimentary.

11. Fertilization is internal, the male having a protrusible copulatory organ; reproduction may be oviparous, ovoviviparous, or viviparous.

described as "popular" terrarium animals, and they will be discussed here only briefly. Information on the captive care of these creatures is obviously sparse, and experimental husbandry should only be carried out by

Note the beautiful yellow striping on this *Ichthyophis kohtaoensis*. Photo by Dr. W. E. Burgess.

There may or may not be an aquatic larval stage.

Due to their relative obscurity, caecilians cannot be

experienced terrarium enthusiasts. However, some caecilians do reasonably well in captivity if given optimum conditions. The burrowing species require a clean, loose, damp substrate, which should be preferably sterile at the outset. It should be well drained and ventilated to prevent build-up of carbon dioxide, carbon monoxide, methane, or other potentially dangerous gases. Aquatic species must have a clean aquarium; a land area may be a good idea, though fully aquatic species will not use or need it. Being tropical, most species should thrive at temperatures from 23-27°C (73-81°F). Most species will take invertebrates of one type or another.

Caecilia has over 30 burrowing species native to Central and South America. *C. gracilis* from tropical South America reaches 45 cm (18 in) in length and is uniformly purple or lilac in color. *C. thompsoni* from Colombia measures up to 120 cm (4 ft) and is sooty brown to black above, gray on the flanks, and dark again beneath; the front of the head is cream to white.

Ichthyophis is a genus containing over 30 species native to Southeast Asia. *I. tricolor*, from southeastern India, grows to 30 cm (12 in). It is violet brown above and white below with a dark-edged yellow stripe along the flanks. Very similar species from Southeast Asia sometimes are seen for sale.

Typhlonectes is a genus containing six (several doubtfully distinct) aquatic species. *T. compressicauda* is found from the Guianas through Brazil to Peru and reaches a maximum length of 60 cm (24 in). It is more or less uniformly brown. The very similar Colombian species *T. natans* is more slender and a solid glossy blue-black in color. It is fairly common in US pet shops at times. Keep it in a warm aquarium; feed on tubifex worms, bloodworms, chopped shrimp, etc.

Index

Bold page numbers indicate photographs